Daily *warm-ups*

COMMONLY CONFUSED WORDS

William W. Gentile, Sr.

WALCH PUBLISHING

1   2   3   4   5   6   7   8   9   10
ISBN 0-8251-4630-5
Copyright © 2003
J. Weston Walch, Publisher
P.O. Box 658 • Portland, Maine 04104-0658
walch.com
Printed in the United States of America

The *Daily Warm-Ups* series is a wonderful way to turn extra classroom minutes into valuable learning time. The 180 quick activities—one for each day of the school year—review, practice, and teach commonly confused and misused words. These daily activities may be used at the very beginning of class to get students into learning mode, near the end of class to make good educational use of that transitional time, in the middle of class to shift gears between lessons—or whenever else you have minutes that now go unused.

Daily Warm-Ups are easy-to-use reproducibles—simply photocopy the day's activity and distribute it. Or make a transparency of the activity and project it on the board. You may want to use the activities for extra-credit points or as a check on the language arts skills that are built and acquired over time.

However you choose to use them, *Daily Warm-Ups* are a convenient and useful supplement to your regular lesson plans. Make every minute of your class time count!

accept, except

accept (vb)—to receive willingly

Example: John **accepted** the trophy on behalf of the entire team.

except (prep)—but; excluding

Example: Everyone **except** Beth went out for pizza after the dance.

Circle the proper word to make the sentence correct.

1. Grace was humble as she (accepted, excepted) the award for most valuable player.

2. My parents will not (accept, except) any excuses for breaking curfew.

3. All of the boys (accept, except) George were on time for the meeting.

4. Malcolm will (accept, except) your package from UPS when it arrives.

5. All of my children have blue eyes (accept, except) my oldest son, Greg.

1

accept, except

Except can also be a verb.

except (vb)—to leave out; to exclude

> Example: His medical condition **excepted** him from playing badminton.

Write a sentence using the verb **except.** Then write a sentence using **except** as a preposition. Finally, write a sentence using the verb **accept.**

2

advice, advise

advice (n)—helpful suggestion or opinion

> Example: Your **advice** is always welcome because you have good ideas.

advise (vb)—to offer advice or suggestions

> Example: Stan's lawyer **advised** him to remain silent under questioning.

Circle the proper word to make the sentence correct.

1. My (advice, advise) to you is to calm down and count to ten.

2. It is always easier to give (advice, advise) than to follow it.

3. Bill is quick to offer his (advice, advise) on any subject.

4. I strongly (advice, advise) you to check your French homework.

advice, advise

A good way to remember the difference between **advice** and **advise** is to keep in mind that they are pronounced differently. The *s* in **advise** is hard (*advize*), while the *c* in **advice** is soft.

Circle the proper word to make the sentence correct.

1. John was (adviced, advised) to be careful driving in the severe windstorm.

2. Sometimes the best (advice, advise) is complete silence on the subject.

3. Do not (advice, advise) someone if you don't know what is best.

4. There are all kinds of books on the market offering financial (advice, advise).

Write two sentences, one using **advice** and the other using **advise.**

4

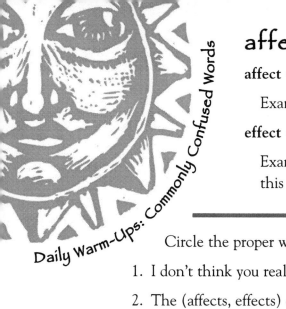

affect, effect

affect (vb)—to influence

> Example: Your criticism **affects** people in a negative way.

effect (n)—the result of some action

> Example: New Englanders have felt the **effect** of Mother Nature this winter.

Circle the proper word to make the sentence correct.

1. I don't think you realize how your comments (affect, effect) your friends.

2. The (affects, effects) of the storm were disastrous along the Louisiana coast.

3. That medicine did have an (affect, effect) on my headache.

5

affect, effect

Effect can also be a verb, although it is used rarely.

effect (vb)—to bring about; to achieve

Example: Through the efforts of Sarah Brady, some gun control measures have been **effected.**

Circle the proper word to make the sentence correct.

1. Congress (affected, effected) a plan to lower the cost of prescription drugs.

2. Don't let your feelings (affect, effect) your usually good judgment.

3. The football team was most (affected, effected) by the new rules.

Write three sentences. Use **affect** once, and then use **effect** as a noun and as a verb.

6

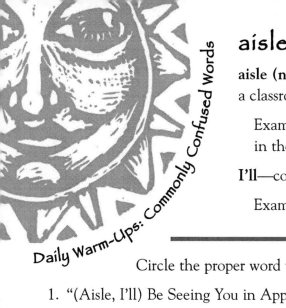

aisle, I'll

aisle (n)—a walkway between or along sections of a theater, a classroom, or the like

> Example: Jake walked up and down the **aisles** trying to find a seat in the stadium.

I'll—contraction of *I will*

> Example: **I'll** keep my promises if I am elected class president.

Circle the proper word to make the sentence correct.

1. "(Aisle, I'll) Be Seeing You in Apple Blossom Time" is an old ballad.

2. There is a question as to whether or not (aisle, I'll) be able to complete the job.

3. Heather looked absolutely beautiful as she walked down the church (aisle, I'll).

4. (Aisle, I'll) give it my very best effort, as I always do.

7

aisle, I'll, isle

isle (n)—a small island; also used to refer to any island regardless of its size

> Example: The **isle** named Capricorn is a mythological land of beauty and intrigue.

Circle the proper word to make the sentence correct.

1. Bermuda is an (aisle, I'll, isle) I have always wanted to visit.

2. The (aisle, I'll, isle) between the last row of seats and the window is too narrow.

3. Ireland is often referred to as the "Emerald (Aisle, I'll, Isle)."

4. Blake tripped Teresa as she walked down the (aisle, I'll, isle) of the auditorium.

8

all ready, already

all ready (adj)—prepared; completely ready

> Example: The volunteers at the homeless shelter were **all ready** to serve dinner to those waiting in the long line.

already (adv)—before some specified time; previously

> Example: By the time Sylvia arrived at school, classes had **already** begun.

Circle the proper word to make the sentence correct.

1. Clarence had his math homework (all ready, already) to pass in.

2. The math test was for one hour, but Scott had (all ready, already) finished in a half-hour.

3. (All ready, Already) for the prom, Denise discovered a tear in her dress.

4. Kyong had (all ready, already) selected a topic for her research paper.

9

all ready, already

Here's a good way to determine whether you are using **all ready** or **already** correctly in a sentence: Replace the word or phrase with *ready* by itself. If your sentence still means the same thing with a bit less emphasis, you should use **all ready;** if not, **already** is probably correct to use.

Circle the proper word to make the sentence correct.

1. The plans for the outside graduation were (all ready, already) when the storm began.

2. (All ready, Already) to begin the tennis match, Drew took a deep breath and tried to relax.

3. It was (all ready, already) too late to call off the game despite the snow.

4. Cliff had (all ready, already) begun to think about plans for his future.

10

all together, altogether

all together (phrase)—in a group or collectively

Example: The class was **all together** for the last pep rally of the year.

altogether (adv)—wholly, entirely, completely, or thoroughly

Example: After one week, it was **altogether** too late to pass in the written assignment.

Circle the proper word to make the sentence correct.

1. "Let's sing this (all together, altogether) now," pleaded the choral director.

2. The waiting period for college acceptance is (all together, altogether) too long.

3. John held the group (all together, altogether) during the crisis.

4. Sometimes we get (all together, altogether) too moody and offend others.

5. The Student Council was (all together, altogether) too removed from the students' views.

11

all together, altogether

A good way to check whether you have used **altogether** correctly is to replace it with its synonym *entirely*. If the meaning or your sentence is the same, you have probably used **altogether** correctly. If the meaning is different, you probably meant to use **all together.**

Write four sentences. Use the terms **all together** and **altogether** twice each.

12

allude, elude

allude (vb)—to refer indirectly

> Example: The teacher **alluded** to the fact that the previous set of essays was excellent.

elude (vb)—to avoid or escape from a person or a thing

> Example: Hank **eluded** the wrath of his teacher by getting his paper in on time.

Circle the correct words in the following paragraph.

The prisoner who sat before the parole board (alluded, eluded) to the fact that his record as a prisoner was exemplary. Admittedly, he did not (allude, elude) to several incidents where he had been cited for (alluding, eluding) the guards who caught him trying to escape. However, he did (allude, elude) to the many times he had given blood to help fellow inmates. In turn, the parole board reminded him of the several attempts he had made to (allude, elude) his responsibilities in doing his daily assigned chores. They (alluded, eluded) to the reports made by the guards. In addition to reporting his violations of (alluding, eluding) work details, the guards pointed out that he had (alluded, eluded) them five times in his escape attempts. The prisoner was ultimately denied parole.

13

allusion, illusion

allusion (n)—an indirect reference or mentioning of something

Example: The president made several **allusions** to the peace treaty he had negotiated.

illusion (n)—a mistaken perception, impression, or idea

Example: The defendant was under the **illusion** that his guilt was unproved.

Circle the proper word to make the sentence correct.

1. Poets often make (allusions, illusions) to the universe in explaining their theories of life.

2. It is an (allusion, illusion) to think that merely doing the work results in a passing grade.

3. A mirage is a perfect example of an (allusion, illusion).

4. The delegates to the convention had the (allusion, illusion) that the nomination for president was a done deal.

allusion, illusion

The words **allusion** and **allude** are very closely related. While **allusion** is an indirect reference, the verb form of this word, **allude,** means *to refer indirectly*. Also, it might help you to remember that **edude** means to escape or avoid something, and both **elude** and escape start with *e*.

Circle the proper word to make the sentence correct.

1. During his acceptance speech, the candidate made several (allusions, illusions) to the need for tax relief.

2. (Allusions, Illusions) are often very difficult to correct.

3. Most of the students have the (allusion, illusion) that it will be easy to find a good job when they graduate.

4. After several (allusions, illusions) to the correct method, the teacher had the class practice.

15

altar, alter

altar (n)— an elevated structure upon which sacrifices may be offered or before which religious ceremonies may be enacted

Example: Beth and Serge stood at the **altar** to recite their wedding vows.

alter (v)—to change or modify

Example: Thia **altered** her plans to accommodate her roommate's schedule.

16

Circle the proper word to make the sentence correct.

1. Sometimes we sacrifice truth on the (altar, alter) of convenience.

2. All together, there were seventeen (altars, alters) in the cathedral.

3. Raymond would not (altar, alter) his views on capital punishment to please the crowd.

4. A photographer often must (altar, alter) her angle in order to capture the correct light.

altar, alter

Alter can also mean *to adjust for a better fit; to tailor.*

Circle the correct words in the following paragraph.

As she walked down the aisle of the church toward the (altar, alter) where she was to be married, Hazel was so happy that she had (altared, altered) her gown. Her mother had insisted, and Hazel complied. However, she would not (altar, alter) her plans to honeymoon in the tropics as her mother also wished. "After all, Mother," said Hazel, "this is my wedding, and I can't (altar, alter) everything to suit you and your dreams." Little did Hazel know that because of a severe storm, she would (altar, alter) her travel plans for her honeymoon, too.

17

among, between

among (prep)—surrounded by; in the number or class of (generally refers to more than two persons or things)

Example: **Among** the triplets, Gary was the largest at birth.

between (prep)—in common to; shared by (generally refers to two persons or things)

Example: It is difficult to decide **between** Jack and Joe for prom king.

Circle the proper word to make the sentence correct.

1. (Among, Between) the five of you, you ought to be able to come up with a solution.

2. It is difficult for two people to keep a secret (among, between) them and not tell others.

3. The twins were able to divide the candy (among, between) themselves.

4. To paraphrase Ben Franklin, three can keep a secret (among, between) themselves if two of them are dead.

18

among, between

Many people think that **between** may *only* be used in the case of two items and **among** in the case of more than two. But **between** really expresses a one-to-one relationship regardless of the number of items involved.

> Example: We are working for peace **between** nations. (The number of nations isn't specified, but the idea is that peace will exist **between** pairs of nations everywhere.)

On the other hand, **among** expresses distribution.

> Example: We shared the food **among** the starving cats.

Circle the proper word to make the sentence correct.

1. Please decide who (among, between) the four of you will speak for the group.

2. (Among, Between) you, me, and the lamppost, I've never been a big fan of his movies.

3. You must decide (among, between) going home or staying for extra help.

4. (Among, Between) the many choices you have after graduation are working, going into the armed services, or attending college.

19

angry, mad

angry (adj)—feeling or showing hostility or resentment

Example: The thing that made Elena **angry** was her inability to express her feelings.

mad (adj)—suffering from a disease of the mind; insane

Example: People suffering from rabies often go **mad** and need to be put in restraints.

Circle the correct words in the following paragraph.

Let me tell you, I am really (angry with, mad at) you this time! I just finished reading some of Poe's short stories, and your analysis of him and some of his characters is way off. Now, I agree with you that the old man in "The Tell-Tale Heart" is rather strange and possibly (angry, mad). All signs point to his having lost his mind, and the character in the "The Masque of the Red Death" was also a bit strange. However, he was hardly (angry, mad)! He was just (angry, mad) with the way the nobility treated the common people at that time.

angry, mad

Although it has become common to use **mad** to mean **angry,** it is not acceptable for formal writing. For written work, avoid using **mad** when you really mean **angry.**

Circle the correct words in the following paragraph.

Now think about Roderick in "The Fall of the House of Usher." He was undoubtedly as (angry, mad) as anyone who had lost his mind could be. In fact, his sister Madeline seemed (angry with, mad at) the world and was determined to make poor Roderick pay for her own mental imbalance or (anger, madness). Then I found out Poe himself may very well have been (angry, mad). He had all the symptoms. Who goes to a friend's mother's grave every day for a year to mourn? You say his characters are (angry, mad), imbalanced, and insane. I say they reflect the author, who may have been as (angry, mad) as the characters he created.

21

ante, anti

ante (prefix)—before

Example: The **ante**room to the main dining room was often where guests were greeted.

anti (prefix)—against

Example: *Uncle Tom's Cabin* led to a wave of **anti**slavery sentiment in the United States.

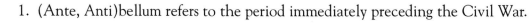

Circle the proper word to make the sentence correct.

1. (Ante, Anti)bellum refers to the period immediately preceding the Civil War.

2. Jerome has always supported (ante, anti)poverty legislation.

3. Proposed (ante, anti)gun legislation angers some hunters.

4. (Ante, Anti)diluvian literally means "before the flood"—the one Noah escaped from in his ark.

5. Marty was accused of being (ante, anti)social when he refused to go to the party.

22

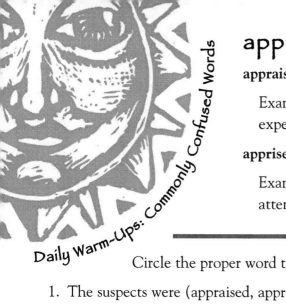

appraise, apprise

appraise (v)—to evaluate

> Example: Julia took a jade figurine, the family heirloom, to an expert to have it **appraised.**

apprise (v)—to inform or cause to know

> Example: Followers of the Great Kuhana were **apprised** of the attempt to kidnap him.

Circle the proper word to make the sentence correct.

1. The suspects were (appraised, apprised) of their rights prior to their arrest.

2. The generals (appraised, apprised) the weather conditions before entering into battle.

3. It is my duty to get to the truth by (appraising, apprising) all of the facts in the case.

4. A reputable jeweler can (appraise, apprise) you of the worth of your engagement ring.

5. In fact, that same jeweler could (appraise, apprise) all of your gemstones.

23

as, like

as (conj)—in or to the same degree; in the same manner (introduces a subordinate or dependent clause)

Example: Jesse won the big race just **as** he had done the year before.

like (prep)—similar to; in the manner of (introduces a prepositional phrase)

Example: You know, you look just **like** your mother.

Note: Do not use **like** to introduce (begin) a clause.

24

Circle the proper word to make the sentence correct.

1. Don't do what I do; do (as, like) I say.

2. The crowd applauded and screamed loudly (as, like) hometown fans usually do.

3. The audience swooned in unison (as, like) a chorus at Ali's portrayal of the dying swan.

4. (As, Like) I said, not many people appreciate your crude remarks.

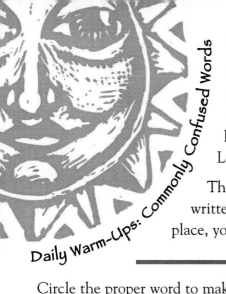

as, like

Many people use the word **like** in spoken English to provide emphasis, to fill up pauses, or to avoid more lengthy word choices such as "on the other hand." For many people, the spoken use of **like** has become repetitive and annoying (for example: "I, **like,** spoke to Louisa on the phone, and she was, **like,** really happy about the game").

The use of **like** for padding speech has led many people to discard it for written work, often unnecessarily. Since you might incorrectly put **as** in its place, you should understand how **like** is used correctly.

Circle the proper word to make the sentence correct.

1. (As, Like) Mary and Betty, Janice had a glorious voice.

2. There is nothing (as, like) a big plate of spaghetti and meatballs to satisfy a big appetite.

3. The mess strewn about the yard looked (as, like) the work of raccoons.

4. The car was ground up (as, like) hamburg after the head-on collision.

25

assay, essay

assay (vb)—to examine or analyze; to judge the quality of

Example: In an attempt to be sure, the military **assayed** the enemy's troop strength.

Example: The jeweler **assayed** the gold in the antique watch.

essay (n)—a short literary composition on a particular theme or subject

Example: In his **essay** on the *E. coli* virus, the author noted the dangers of raw meat.

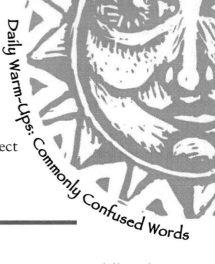

Circle the proper word to make the sentence correct.

1. It is important to turn in your (assays, essays) on time to receive full credit.

2. I (assayed, essayed) the situation and then made a decision to cancel my subscription.

3. Mr. Rentfro, our local jeweler, (assayed, essayed) the value of Jill's diamond bracelet.

4. Now we will concentrate on writing academic (assays, essays) of five paragraphs.

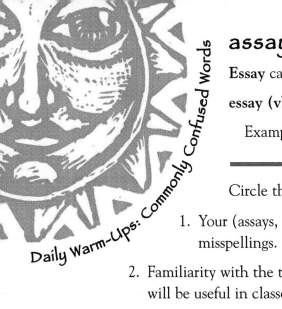

assay, essay

Essay can also be a verb.

essay (vb)—to try

> Example: Marco **essayed** a new dance step in his flamenco class.

Circle the proper word to make the sentence correct.

1. Your (assays, essays) are too long and loaded with wordiness and misspellings.

2. Familiarity with the traditional five-paragraph (assay, essay) will be useful in classes that require you to take written tests.

3. Jean (assayed, essayed) the rock-climbing wall after carefully (assaying, essaying) how difficult it was.

4. (Assay, Essay) every course of action before you embark upon one.

27

bad, badly

bad (adj)—not good in manner or degree; unpleasant, unattractive, unfavorable, spoiled

Example: Alphonse made a very **bad** choice when he decided to leave school early.

Example: I felt really **bad** about your having to rewrite your essay five times.

badly (adv)—in a defective, an incorrect, or an undesirable way; in an unsatisfactory, inadequate, or unskilled manner

Example: The trumpet part was played so **badly** that the performance was ruined.

28

Circle the proper word to make the sentence correct.

1. The stagnant water smelled (bad, badly) from the decaying leaves.

2. The lobsters went (bad, badly) after sitting in the barrel for six hours without ice.

3. The chess team played so (bad, badly) they finished in last place in the tournament.

4. Charles felt (bad, badly) about passing up the opportunity for a large scholarship.

bad, badly

When referring to emotions, one feels **bad,** not **badly.** Because **badly** is an adverb, by definition it must refer to the verb *feel* (since adverbs modify verbs, adjectives, or other adverbs). Thus, to *feel **badly*** would mean to have a poor sense of touch.

Circle the proper word to make the sentence correct.

1. Jasmine's choice to attend West Point was not a (bad, badly) decision.

2. I play the piano quite (bad, badly), but I enjoy it too much to stop trying.

3. After having played (bad, badly) in their first game, the football team came together and went undefeated for the remainder of the season.

4. I don't care how (bad, badly) the excuse sounds, it is entirely true.

29

Review

Circle the proper word to make the sentence correct.

1. They were used to following directions (as, like) they were trained to do.

2. Javier (accepted, excepted) Brian's explanation, not realizing he was trying to (allude, elude) punishment.

3. (Aisle, I'll, Isle) see you (all together, altogether) at the science fair.

4. Your mistaken ideas result from an (allusion, illusion) you have about the correct process.

5. Shana would not let the morose mood of the others (affect, effect) her cheery disposition.

6. Greg was careful not to (advice, advise) Peter about next year's course selections.

7. Later, I felt (bad, badly) about the fact that I (appraised, apprised) Jermaine of his surprise party.

8. Jenny (assayed, essayed) the value of the Internet for research purposes in her informative (assay, essay).

30

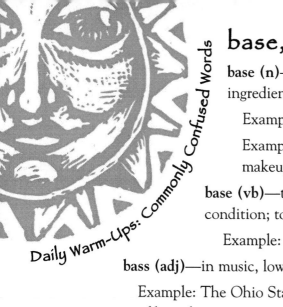

base, bass

base (n)—the bottom support of anything; the principal element or ingredient of anything; center or area of operations

Example: The **base** of the statue was made of Italian marble.

Example: Laura used a **base** of light powder before applying her makeup.

base (vb)—to make or form a foundation for; to make as a fact or condition; to station, place, or situate

Example: Always **base** your opinions on solid facts.

bass (adj)—in music, low in pitch; of the lowest pitch range

Example: The Ohio State Band is famous for its large number of **bass** drums.

Circle the correct words in the following paragraph.

Six members of the air squadron at the air force (base, bass) in Colorado were on leave. They decided to go backpacking. On the way to their campsite, they became aware of the (base, bass) call of wild animals. Jerome, who sang (base, bass) in the glee club at the (base, bass), tried to imitate the animals, but his voice was far too deep.

31

base, bass

Base and **bass** have other forms and meanings.

base (adj)—serving or forming as a base; morally low, dishonorable

Example: The employer used the annual cost-of-living index to raise his workers' **base** salaries.

bass (n)—(pronounced with a short *a*) a kind of fish

Example: **Bass** put up a good fight and are fun to catch.

Circle the correct words in the following paragraph.

32

The next day, the air squadron members went fishing for (base, bass). When they reached the (base, bass) of the river, they noticed storm clouds forming on the horizon, but they ignored the clouds because the temptation to catch large (base, bass) was too strong. Suddenly, Jerome let out a roar and uttered some (base, bass) remarks—he had just been stung by a hornet. Just then, lightening struck close by. The men decided to return to (base, bass) to escape further trouble.

because, since

because (conj)—for the reason that

Example: I didn't get my yard work finished **because** it rained all weekend.

since (conj)—in view of the fact that

Example: **Since** the rain kept me from mowing the lawn, I sat on the couch and read a book.

Note: As you can see from the examples, the distinction between **because** and **since** is subtle. Use **because** when you want to express a direct cause-and-effect relationship. Use **since** when there is a logical connection between two events, but the first didn't cause the second.

Circle the proper word to make the sentence correct.

1. I was tardy today (because, since) I missed the bus.

2. Julia decided to see the doctor (because, since) she had health coverage.

3. Sam's poodle didn't get a lot of exercise, especially (because, since) she shied away from other dogs.

4. Sam's poodle shies away from other dogs (because, since) she was bitten when she was a puppy.

33

because, since

Because is always a conjunction; **since,** however, can be an adverb.

since (adv)—before now; from a point in the past until now

Example: Maria moved to New York to attend college and has lived there ever **since.**

If you remember **since** as an adverb, it will help you use the word correctly. In both of its uses, **since** refers to a time before the present that is linked to the present, whereas **because** signifies cause and effect.

Circle the proper word to make the sentence correct.

1. I have enjoyed sailing ever (because, since) I took a lesson at a local yacht club.

2. Maurice didn't pass the test (because, since) he didn't study.

3. (Because, Since) we had already purchased the tickets, we decided to take time for dinner before the concert.

4. (Because, Since) he joined the hockey team, my brother has been doing nothing but practicing skating backward.

beside, besides

beside (prep)—next to; by the side of

Example: Lee stood **beside** Robin as they exchanged wedding vows.

besides (prep)—in addition to

Example: **Besides** cake, my favorite dessert is ice cream.

Write five sentences. Use **beside** in three of them, and use **besides** in the other two.

35

beside, besides

Besides can also be an adverb.

besides (adv)—moreover; as well

Example: We can't move today because the truck isn't available; **besides**, I haven't completely packed yet.

Write three sentences. Use **beside** in the first, **besides** as a preposition in the second, and **besides** as an adverb in the third.

36

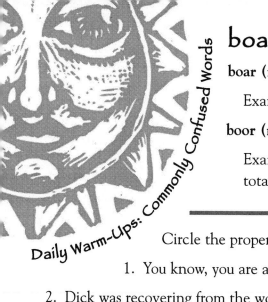

boar, boor

boar (n)—a male pig; a wild pig

Example: Steve and Delores went on a safari to hunt wild **boar.**

boor (n)—a crude person with rude, clumsy manners

Example: With his incessant muttering of racial slurs, Pete was a total **boor** to his guests.

Circle the proper word to make the sentence correct.

1. You know, you are a complete (boar, boor) when you start with your ethnic jokes.

2. Dick was recovering from the wound inflicted on him by a wild (boar, boor).

3. Morgan's sharp put-downs gave her the reputation of a (boar, boor).

37

boar, boor, bore

bore (vb)—to make a hole in or through, with (or as if with) a drill or similar tool; to make by drilling, digging, or burrowing

> Example: In order to complete the birdhouse, Al **bored** three large holes in the front panel.

bore (vb)—to tire with dullness, repetitiveness, or tediousness

> Example: Please do not **bore** me with your excuses for being late.

bore (n)—someone or something that bores

> Example: It is such a **bore** when my dad talks about his hobbies.

Note: **Bore** is also the past tense of the verb *bear*, to carry.

Circle the proper word to make the sentence correct.

1. The termites (boar, boor, bore) holes in the wooden foundations of the house.

2. Students were never (boared, boored, bored) in Mr. Mohammed's biology class.

3. Jill plans to (boar, boor, bore) three holes in the cabinet to accommodate the brass fixtures.

4. Ron (boar, boor, bore) the criticism of his sculpture quite well.

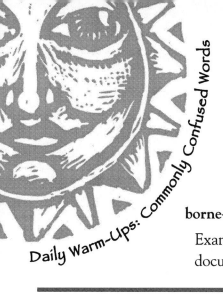

born, borne

born (adj)—brought forth by birth; possessing from birth the quality stated

> Example: Maggie's twins were **born** right after midnight on January 23.

> Example: Danny was a **born** athlete, especially talented in basketball.

borne—past participle of *to bear*; carried, supported, endured

> Example: The trials and tribulations **borne** by American Indians are well documented in American history.

Circle the proper word to make the sentence correct.

1. (Born, Borne) on July 4, Ben celebrated his birthday along with the birth of the nation.

2. The entire weight of the two boys was (born, borne) by the horse.

3. Gloria, a (born, borne) actress, won a full scholarship to New York University.

4. In a huge basket, the eight puppies were (born, borne) to the animal shelter for adoption.

brake, break

brake (v)—to slow down

Example: Jeremy skidded and almost hit the road sign, but he **braked** the car in time.

break (v)—to separate into parts, often with suddenness or violence

Example: If you pour extremely hot water into a glass, you will probably **break** it.

Note: The present, past, and perfect participles of **brake** are *brake, braked, braked*. The present, past, and perfect participles of **break** are *break, broke, broken*.

40

Circle the proper word to make the sentence correct.

1. Drive slowly enough so that when you (brake, break), the car will not jolt forward.

2. Do not (brake, break) the lines of communication with your friends over frivolous matters.

3. Each time you (brake, break) a promise, your credibility comes into question.

4. The bus driver (braked, broke) suddenly to avoid hitting a family of opossum.

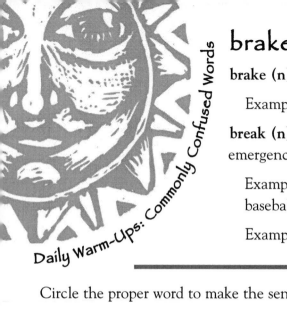

brake, break

brake (n)—a device used to slow down

Example: When the car is skidding, do not slam on the **brakes.**

break (n)—the result of a breaking; a fracture; an interruption; an emergence (as in *the **break** of day*)

Example: The **break** in John's arm healed in time for him to play baseball.

Example: We expected to go to Cancun for spring **break.**

Circle the proper word to make the sentence correct.

1. A (brake, break) in the telephone service was caused by a violent hurricane.

2. I was not prepared for the expense of repairing the (brakes, breaks) on my car.

3. Everyone enjoyed a (brake, break) in the hot weather.

4. Mom's arrival put a (brake, break) on our little chemistry experiment.

41

buy, by

buy (v)—to acquire in exchange for money; to purchase

Example: Every year, my cousin **buys** a new car.

by (prep)—next to; with the use of or through; not later than

Example: Paul walked **by** the cafeteria and entered the gymnasium.

Example: **By** working hard, Josie earned enough money to go skiing in Aspen.

Example: I expect every essay to be passed in **by** the deadline.

Circle the correct words in the following paragraph.

42

Alvin and his golf partner, Lindsay, stood (buy, by) the counter in the course's pro shop. They were waiting for the cashier to return so they could (buy, by) some new golf balls for the tournament. Lindsay said to Alvin, "If that guy isn't back (buy, by) the time I count to twenty, I'm just going to use the balls I have." Alvin agreed, saying, "We need to get to the first tee (buy, by) the time they start drawing names."

buy, by, bye

bye (n)—in sports, the position of one who draws no opponent for a round in a tournament and so advances to the next round

---

Circle the correct words in the following paragraph.

Alvin and Lindsay stood (buy, by, bye) the scorers table and realized early on that they would draw a (buy, by, bye) for the first round of the tournament. Alvin decided he would (buy, by, bye) four tickets to the banquet that evening so they could take their spouses. They left the golf course and went in different directions to get home, Alvin (buy, by, bye) the freeway and Lindsay (buy, by, bye) Main Avenue.

43

capital, capitol

capital (n)—a city or town that is the official seat of government in a country or state; an uppercase letter of the alphabet; wealth or resources

Example: Sacramento is the **capital** of California.

Example: Always use a **capital** letter to begin a sentence.

Example: When a company runs out of **capital,** it generally files for bankruptcy.

capitol (n)—primarily, the building in Washington, D.C., where Congress sits, or similar buildings used by state legislators

Example: At the **capitol** in Augusta, the legislators pass laws that affect Maine people.

Note: When referring to the capitol in Washington, the word is uppercase.

44

Circle the proper word to make the sentence correct.

1. I have a hard time differentiating between your lowercase and (capital, capitol) letters.

2. I have invested all of my (capital, capitol) in mutual funds.

3. On the steps of the (capital, capitol) in Texas, the governor took his oath of office.

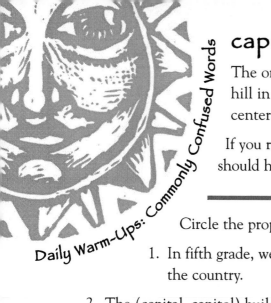

capital, capitol

The original **capitol** building was the Temple of Jupiter on Capitoline hill in Rome. This was the political and religious center of the city.

If you remember that **capitol** always and only refers to a *building*, you should have no problem with these terms.

Circle the proper word to make the sentence correct.

1. In fifth grade, we had to learn the names of every state (capital, capitol) in the country.

2. The (capital, capitol) building of every state is where the legislators meet to make laws.

3. The poet E. E. Cummings often did not use (capital, capitol) letters in his poems.

45

cent, scent

cent (n)—a bronze-colored coin of the United States worth $\frac{1}{100}$ of a dollar

Example: Joseph charged one **cent** for a piece of candy.

scent (n)—a distinctive odor, especially when agreeable; an odor left in passing by means of which an animal or a person may be traced; the sense of smell

Example: The **scent** of lilacs filled the air when spring was finally here.

Example: Bloodhounds have a natural ability to follow the **scent** of humans.

46

Circle the correct words in the following paragraph.

"This is a fraudulent insurance claim, and the company will not pay so much as one (cent, scent) to your clients," said the lawyer. "We were able to smell the (cent, scent) of the scheme from the beginning." The (cent, scent) of cigar smoke began to fill the room as the opposition began to sweat. They knew the reputation of Juan Gonzalez's reputation.

cent, scent, sent

scent (v)—to smell; to hunt by smell; to detect as if by smelling

Example: The dogs **scented** the trail of the escaped prisoner.

sent (v)—past tense of the verb *to send*

Example: The detectives **sent** the evidence to a crime lab to be examined by forensic scientists.

Circle the correct words in the following paragraph.

Gonzalez then said he had (cent, scent, sent) a report to the attorney general about the insurance claim. The team of opposed lawyers silently (cent, scent, sent) signals to each other for compromise. They announced they would reduce their claim by half. "Nonsense," replied Gonzalez. He turned to his associate and whispered, "Do you smell the (cent, scent, sent) of defeat in that offer? I don't think we'll have to pay a red (cent, scent, sent)."

47

© 2003 J. Weston Walch, Publisher

choose, chose

choose (vb)—to decide on and pick out; to select; to prefer

Example: When you **choose** the topic for this essay, be sure you state your thesis clearly.

chose—past tense of **choose**

Example: Alex **chose** all of his electives in the area of science, his intended major.

Circle the proper word to make the sentence correct.

1. We all hope to (choose, chose) friends who will stand by us in times of need.

2. After deliberating for a few minutes, Maria (choose, chose) the most obvious route home.

3. In college, one usually (chooses, choses) a major after the first year.

4. Anyone who drives after consuming alcohol is (choosing, chosing) to flirt with disaster.

5. Hattie (choose, chose) several new books to read on her trip to Ireland.

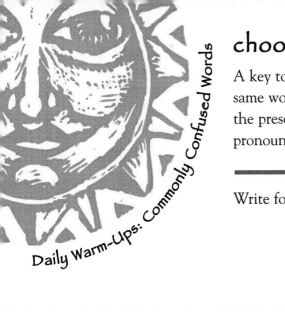

choose, chose

A key to remembering the difference between these two forms of the same word is to keep in mind how they are pronounced. **Choose,** the present, is pronounced *chüz,* whereas the past tense, **chose,** is pronounced *chōz.*

Write four sentences. Use **choose** in two and **chose** in two.

49

cite, sight

cite (vb)—to quote a passage, a book, an author, or another source, especially as an authority; to summon officially to appear in court; to commend

Example: You must **cite** several sources as you write your research paper.

Example: **Cited** for speeding in a school zone, Brenda appeared in court and was fined.

Example: Carlos was **cited** for his outstanding service to his community.

sight (vb)—to observe within one's field of vision; to take aim at

Example: Siegfried **sighted** the tall ships as they began their entrance into Boston Harbor.

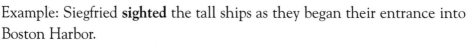

50

Write four sentences. Use **cite** in two and **sight** in two.

cite, sight, site

sight (n)—the power of seeing; a view; a field of vision

Example: Brad momentarily lost his **sight** from the pepper spray used by the intruder.

Example: Clara was overcome by the **sight** of the city's poorest section.

site (n)—the exact location or position of something; the position or location of a town building, and so forth, especially in relation to its environment

Example: The dump **site** reeked of rotting garbage.

Circle the correct words in the following paragraph.

They encountered quite a (cite, sight, site) as they arrived at the (cite, sight, site) of the devastation created by the tornado. News reporters were quickly on the scene and (cited, sighted, sited) several sources as saying that they had (cited, sighted, sited) the dark funnel cloud on the horizon only minutes before it tore its way across the (cite, sight, site) they were standing on. The (cite, sight, site) distressed the most seasoned veteran reporters, and they were (cited, sighted, sited) leaving the (cite, sight, site) hurriedly.

51

click, clique

click (n)—a brief, sharp, nonresonant sound

Example: Edgar was frightened as he heard the **click** of the door closing behind him.

clique (n)—an exclusive group of people

Example: **Cliques** are usually formed by people with similar interests.

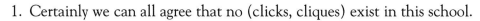

Circle the proper word to make the sentence correct.

1. Certainly we can all agree that no (clicks, cliques) exist in this school.

2. Forty (clicks, cliques) of the timer sounded before a terrified Jennifer let out her breath.

3. (Clicks, Cliques) seem to be a fact of life for any large organization.

4. Many (clicks, cliques) are intolerant and have narrow views of the world they live in.

click, clique

Click can also be a verb.

click (vb)—to make a brief, sharp, nonresonant sound; to fit exactly; to hit it off; to select something by clicking

   Example: The key **clicked** softly as it turned in the lock.

Note: Some people might confuse **click** in its meaning of *hit it off* with the word **clique.** The words, however, are not related.

Write three sentences. Use **clique** in one, **click** as a noun in one, and **click** as a verb in the last.

53

close, close

close (v)—to move (a door, a gate, and so forth) so as to bar passage; to bring to an end; to conclude discussion about

Example: Maximo wanted to **close** the door in the salesman's face, but he was too polite.

close (adj)—confined; strict; familiar; being near in time or space

Example: My house is **close** to the school I attend.

Write four sentences. Use the verb **close** in two and the adjective **close** in the other two.

54

close, close

The difficulty with these words is that they are pronounced differently. The verb **close** is pronounced with a hard *s* (*z*) and the adjective **close** is pronounced with a soft *s*. This confusion often leads people to read the words incorrectly.

Circle the correct pronunciation in the following paragraph.

Teresa loves to ride her bicycle to work, especially because her work is so close (*cloz, clos*) to her home. On some mornings, she has close (*cloz, clos*) calls with people in cars. Like all good cyclists, Teresa rides her bike on the road, quite close (*cloz, clos*) to traffic. Sometimes people in parked cars open their doors and don't close (*cloz, clos*) them quickly enough, and she comes close (*cloz, clos*) to running into them. When she gets to work, she often waits for a coworker to open and close (*cloz, clos*) the door for her—it's pretty difficult to hold a door and haul in a bike at the same time.

55

cloths, clothes

cloths (n)—plural of *cloth*; pieces of fabric

Example: Always use soft **cloths** when polishing your car.

clothes (n)—apparel; attire

Example: Jason was always complaining that he never had any **clothes** to wear.

Circle the proper word to make the sentence correct.

1. The quilt Aurelie made consisted of old pieces of (cloths, clothes) she had saved.

2. Shopping for new school (cloths, clothes) in the fall, was fun for Ali and his mom.

3. Fred looked for very absorbent (cloths, clothes) for drying the outside windows.

4. Natasha worked hard to design new styles in her line of summer (cloths, clothes).

56

cloths, clothe, clothes

clothe (vb)—to put clothes on; to dress

Example: A dresser's job is to **clothe** another, often a movie star.

Circle the proper word to make the sentence correct.

1. It took a great deal of money for the Smiths to (cloths, clothe, clothes) their five children.

2. In a hardware store, you can buy a big box of (cloths, clothe, clothes) for a reasonable price.

3. The synagogue ran a drive to collect winter coats to (cloths, clothe, clothes) the disadvantaged children in the community.

4. Spring (cloths, clothe, clothes) are already on sale, although it's still midwinter.

57

© 2003 J. Weston Walch, Publisher

coarse, course

coarse (adj)—rough or crude

Example: Rice is very **coarse** in its raw state until it is milled.

course (n)—the route taken by something that moves, as a river; duration; a mode of action or behavior; a body of prescribed studies; a part of a meal served as a unit at one time

Example: Jeff was unsure just what **course** of action he would take after his false arrest.

Example: Jill took three English **courses** to fulfill requirements for her major.

Example: The first **course** of their meal was a delicious Caesar salad.

58

Circle the correct words in the following paragraph.

Bethany and Craig sat down to enjoy a seven-(coarse, course) meal before going to the theater. They began with two appetizers, one made of fried shrimp and the other of smoked salmon lightly coated with (coarse, course) pepper. As the entrée of beef Wellington was served, they changed the (coarse, course) of conversation to the decorations on the walls of the restaurant. There were several collages of (coarse, course) cloth just over the mantle of the fireplace, next to which was a painting of pioneers following the (coarse, course) of the Oregon Trail. The time seemed to fly by, and before long, they were enjoying dessert, their final (coarse, course).

coarse, course

Course can also be a verb.

course (vb)—to pass rapidly along as on a path; to pursue (especially to hunt with dogs)

Example: In pursuit of their prey, the foxhounds **coursed** down the hill and over a stone wall.

Circle the proper word to make the sentence correct.

1. When training for a race, I change the (coarse, course) I take periodically to challenge myself.

2. The blood from the transfusion began to (coarse, course) through the patient's bloodstream.

3. Sheila took a fly fishing (coarse, course) at her local bait shop, and now she loves the sport.

4. The river starts as a whitewater (coarse, course), but it widens and begins to (coarse, course) more gently as it nears the ocean.

59

Review

Circle the proper word to make the sentence correct.

1. (Because, Since) I had bought brown sugar the previous weekend, I decided to make chocolate chip cookies rather than brownies.

2. Cornelia (based, bassed) her decision to learn the (base, bass) guitar on the fact that her best friend, Andy, played lead guitar in his band.

3. Gwyneth's canoe was (born, borne) off by the river's current straight toward the rocky shallows.

4. I'm going to put the (brakes, breaks) on the conversation if you begin to (boar, boor, bore) people with your rambling stories.

5. If you plan to start a business of your own, remember that you will need some start-up (capital, capitol).

6. The freshly baked apple pie (cent, scent, sent) a plume of steam and a sweet (cent, scent, sent) throughout the house.

7. Yesterday, the town council met to finally (choose, chose) the (cite, sight, site) of the new administrative building.

8. The popular (click, clique) at my school tends to ostracize other students if they don't wear the most fashionable (cloths, clothe, clothes).

60

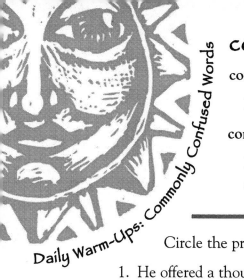

complement, compliment

complement (n)—that which makes whole or complete

Example: The dessert was a fine **complement** to a delicious meal.

compliment (n)—respect, affection, or esteem

Example: As an ambassador, Sergio paid his **compliments** to the queen.

Circle the proper word to make the sentence correct.

1. He offered a thoughtful (complement, compliment) to the essay finalists.

2. Akira realized his sentence wasn't correct without a (complement, compliment) to complete the last phrase.

3. To vote a rule change, the board of directors needed a full (complement, compliment) of members.

4. A good tip after a meal in a restaurant is a (complement, compliment) to the server.

5. (Complementary, Complimentary) angles make up an entire unit in geometry.

61

complement, compliment

While **complement** and **compliment** are often used as nouns, they can also be used as verbs.

complement (vb)—to make whole or complete

Example: The colorful scarf Eric wore **complemented** his whole ensemble.

compliment (vb)—to show kindness or high regard

Example: Olivia **complimented** Joyce on getting a home run.

Circle the proper word to make the sentence correct.

62

1. Antoine (complemented, complimented) his wardrobe by buying an additional sweater.

2. Beth (complemented, complimented) Gracie for winning the oratory contest.

3. The two angles (complement, compliment) each other; together, they make 90°.

Write two new sentences, one using the verb **complement** and the other using the verb **compliment.**

Which sentence was easier to write? Why?

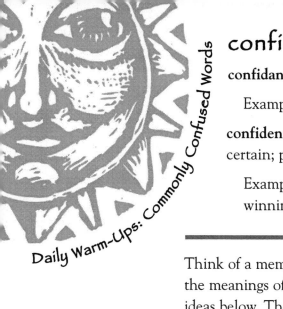

confidant, confident

confidant (n)—a person to whom secrets are or can be entrusted

Example: Guidance counselors often serve as **confidants.**

confident (adj)—having a strong belief or full assurance; sure; certain; positive

Example: I am **confident** that our basketball team will have a winning season this year.

Think of a memory trick or device that you can use to help you remember the meanings of **confidant** and **confident.** Write your ideas below. Then write a short paragraph using both the noun **confidant** and the adjective **confident.**

63

confidant, confident

Remember that the noun **confidant** means a person who can be trusted; the adjective **confident** means certain or sure.

Circle the proper word to make the sentence correct.

1. Juanita was a (confidant, confident) speaker; she was sure she could persuade her classmates with her argument.

2. I was flattered that Jason considered me a (confidant, confident), and I promised not to share his secrets.

3. Lucia was (confidant, confident) that she could trust Mrs. Flannery and tell her what was happening at home.

4. Rebecca became a more (confidant, confident) dancer each time she performed.

64

conscience, conscious

conscience (n)—the sense of recognizing the difference between right and wrong

Example: After stealing the candy in the store, Greg's **conscience** began to bother him.

conscious (adj)—to be aware or alert; knowing

Example: Barry was **conscious** of some other presence in the darkened room.

Circle the proper word to make the sentence correct.

1. Andrea was (conscience, conscious) just before the nurse inserted the needle into her arm.

2. Jack's (conscience, conscious) forced him to own up to his mistake.

3. Some criminals have absolutely no (conscience, conscious) when breaking the law.

4. Zadie's work made her (conscience, conscious) of the utter poverty some people face.

5. Mark's (conscience, conscious) attempts to improve his grade paid off.

65

consul, council, counsel

consul (n)—a diplomat appointed by a government to reside in a foreign country to look after the interests of fellow citizens traveling or doing business there

> Example: The United States **consul** in Vietnam was responsible for helping Greg plan a successful trip.

council (n)—a group that meets to discuss and take action on official matters

> Example: The student **council** meets regularly to discuss the concerns of the school.

> **counsel (n)**—advice

> Example: Briggs received good **counsel** when he was told to cooperate fully.

66

Write three complete sentences, one using **consul,** one using **council,** and the other using **counsel.**

Which sentence was the most difficult to write? Why?

consul, council, counsel

Counsel can also be a verb.

counsel (vb)—to give advice

> Example: Agnes was **counseled** not to give the sources for her newspaper article.

Circle the correct words in the following paragraph.

The town (consul, council, counsel) met to review the possibility of adopting a sister town in India. The (consul, council, counsel) they received from their attorney was to contact the foreign (consul, council, counsel) at the embassy in Bombay to see if the idea was possible. They received a letter a week later from the city (consul, council, counsel) in India, who stated they were excited about the prospects of having a sister town (consul, council, counsel) with whom they could share common problems. The next step for the town (consul, council, counsel) was to contact the United States (consul, council, counsel) again at his official office in India and solicit his direct (consul, council, counsel). At that point, the local (consul, council, counsel) could finalize a decision on the matter.

67

descent, dissent

descent (n)—an act or a process of moving downward; a downward incline; ancestry

Example: The **descent** from the mountain was treacherous because of huge ice fields.

Example: With his entire lineage coming from France, Gil was of French **descent.**

dissent (n)—a difference in sentiment or opinion; disagreement, dissatisfaction; opposition

Example: The opposition's **dissent** was based on the opinions expressed by the president.

dissent (vb)—to disagree; to reject the opinions of another or others

Example: Jedd was the only one who **dissented** with the majority of his political party.

68

Write three complete sentences, one using the noun **descent,** one using the noun **dissent,** and the other using the verb **dissent.**

decent, descent, dissent

Recall that **descent** refers to the process of moving downward; **dissent** as a noun is a difference of opinion; and **dissent** as a verb means to disagree. Now that you are familiar with these words, remember not to confuse them with **decent,** pronounced *dé-sent*.

decent (adj)—conforming to the standard of propriety, good taste, modesty, and so forth, as in behavior or speech; respectable, worthy, adequate, fair, passable, or proper

Example: Standards of **decent** classroom behavior are established by each teacher.

Circle the correct words in the following paragraph.

The hikers began their (decent, descent, dissent) of the mountain when a storm approached. As they began, however, the weather turned (decent, descent, dissent), and some argued that a (decent, descent, dissent) was unnecessary. The (decent, descent, dissent) was short-lived, however, because the hikers realized they were without a (decent, descent, dissent) amount of water. No one (decented, descented, dissented), and the hikers made (decent, descent, dissent) time getting to the bottom of the mountain.

69

desert, dessert

desert (n)—a dry or an arid area

Example: Incredible sandstorms often sweep across the **desert.**

desert (v)—to leave or abandon

Example: The Speaker of the House found his allies **deserted** him when it came to passing the crime bill.

dessert (n)—the sweet food served as the last course of a meal

Example: Fruit can be a refreshing **dessert,** especially in the summer.

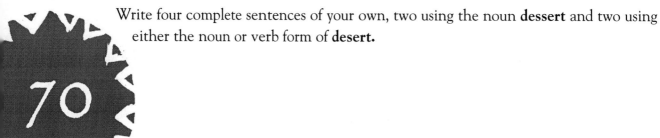

Write four complete sentences of your own, two using the noun **dessert** and two using either the noun or verb form of **desert.**

70

desert, dessert

Recall that the noun **desert** is a dry or an arid area; the noun **dessert** is a dish served at the end of a meal. It may help to remember that you need a second *s* to spell **dessert,** just as you might enjoy a second helping of your favorite sweet treat.

Circle the proper word to make the sentence correct.

1. The bikers (deserted, desserted) their plans to ride because of the lightning storm.

2. The Sahara is one of the largest (deserts, desserts) in the world.

3. My favorite (desert, dessert) is unquestionably strawberry shortcake.

4. We (deserted, desserted) the plan to make pumpkin pie, since we were missing ingredients.

5. Marika was not prepared for the intensely dry, hot climate of the (desert, dessert).

71

device, devise

device (n)—an implement or invention

Example: A Crock-Pot is a **device** used to cook food very slowly.

devise (vb)—to think through or invent; to plan

Example: **Devise** a plan for studying for exams and then follow through with it.

Circle the proper word to make the sentence correct.

1. Chitra used a complicated (device, devise) to solve the problem in physics.

2. The (device, devise) itself was actually made from an erector set Chitra had as a child.

3. She worked hard to (device, devise) a plan to attack the problem.

4. The conclusion she came to was flawed, so Chitra worked to (device, devise) a better approach.

72

dew, do, due

dew (n)—the moisture condensed from the atmosphere, especially at night, and deposited in the form of small drops on any cool surface

Example: The **dew** was heavy and thick, which made the football field slick for the game.

do (vb)—to perform, fulfill, complete, make

Example: If you study, you will **do** your very best on the exam.

due (adj)—payable; owed as a debt; scheduled

Example: The **due** date for the research paper was extended.

Write a short paragraph using **dew, do,** and **due.** Circle each vocabulary word, and write the correct part of speech above it.

73

dew, do, due

While **due** can be used as a adjective, it is also commonly used as a noun.

due (n)—something that is payable or owed as a debt

> Example: Aidan received his **due** when he failed to pass in his essay on *Hamlet*.

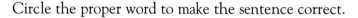

Circle the proper word to make the sentence correct.

1. The (dew, do, due) provides flowers with much needed water when there is a lack of rain.

2. Sasha's library books were long past (dew, do, due).

3. Dave really wanted to (dew, do, due) well on his final examination in biology.

4. Because she had to write an essay that was (dew, do, due), June missed an episode of her favorite television show.

5. (Dew, Do, Due) the easiest math problems first, and then deal with the most difficult.

74

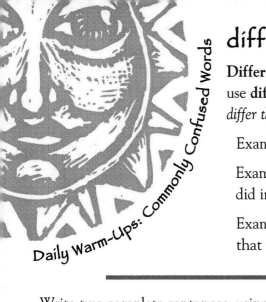

different from, different than

Different from is the proper phrase to use when comparing. Do not use **different than.** One thing differs from *another*; it does not *differ than.*

> Example: Driving sober is quite **different from** driving drunk.

> Example: The problems on the test will be **different from** those we did in the textbook.

> Example: The thought process used in geometry is **different from** that used in algebra.

Write two complete sentences, using **different from** in each one.

75

doesn't, don't

doesn't—contraction of *does not*

Example: Donald **doesn't** always make it to class on time.

Example: He keeps making excuses that he **doesn't** hear the bell.

Example: It **doesn't** make any difference to Ms. Wells, who always gives him detention.

Note: Use **doesn't** *only* with the third person singular words, such as he, she, and it.

don't—contraction of *do not*

Example: Beatrice and Tom **don't** enjoy sports and never attend the games.

Example: Your various excuses **don't** carry any weight with me.

Note: Never use **don't** with the third person singular.

76

Write four complete sentences. Use **doesn't** in two of them and **don't** in the other two.

doesn't, don't

If you're unsure whether to use **doesn't** or **don't,** it may help to take the contraction apart. Consider **does** and **do** by themselves. It may be easier to tell that *she does* sounds right, while *she do* sounds wrong. Therefore, you can determine that *she doesn't* is the correct choice.

Circle the proper word to make the sentence correct.

1. No matter what you say, it (doesn't, don't) make any difference to me.

2. Passing one quiz (doesn't, don't) make you an algebra scholar.

3. The Mississippi River (doesn't, don't) flow through the state of Nevada.

4. Stock market prices (doesn't, don't) usually fluctuate as much as they have recently.

5. The twins really (doesn't, don't) enjoy always being compared to each other.

77

dual, duel

dual (adj)—of or pertaining to two; composed or consisting of two people, items, or parts; having a double nature

Example: It is not always easy to determine the **dual** purposes of a chemical.

duel (n)—a prearranged combat between two persons fought with deadly weapons according to an accepted code or procedure, especially to settle a private quarrel; any contest between two persons or parties

Example: Getting the bill passed in the House became a **duel** between the two parties.

78

Write a short paragraph using both the adjective **dual** and the noun **duel.**

dual, duel

While **duel** can be used as a noun, it is often used as verb.

duel (v)—to fight in a duel; to contest

> Example: Many characters in Shakespeare's plays **dueled** to settle their differences.

Circle the proper word to make the sentence correct.

1. The use of (duals, duels) to settle arguments between two people is outlawed.

2. The talent show contestants (dualed, dueled) each other in a close competition.

3. Like many superheroes, Spider-man has a (dual, duel) persona.

4. The (dual, duel) between Ben and Brandon for first place in the race was the closest of all.

5. The (dual, duel) disk brakes on the Mercedes ended up saving Gayatri's life.

79

each other, one another

Each other is a term used when referring to *only* two persons or things.

> Example: John and Jim are twin brothers and share a bedroom with **each other.**

> Example: Divide into pairs and help **each other** with the difficult word problems.

One another is a term used when referring to *more* than two persons or things.

> Example: The quadruplets were used to helping **one another** with science papers.

> Example: The family members all exchanged e-mails with **one another.**

80

Circle the proper word to make the sentence correct.

1. Brenna and Diane helped (each other, one another) during the long debate.

2. Joe, Naguib, and David helped (each other, one another) during each rebuttal.

3. We are a football team, and we need to work with (each other, one another) on defense.

4. You two are not good for (each other, one another) because of your practical jokes.

Daily Warm-Ups: Commonly Confused Words

elegy, eulogy

elegy (n)—a song or a poem written to mourn or to lament a dead person or persons

Example: Kirsten wrote an **elegy** in memory of her friend Ellie, who died in a car accident.

eulogy (n)—a public tribute, usually in the form of a speech or an oration, often to one who has died

Example: Perhaps the best known **eulogy** is the one Mark Antony wrote in tribute to Caesar.

Write four complete sentences. Use **elegy** in two and **eulogy** in two.

81

elicit, illicit

elicit (v)—to bring out or to draw forth

Example: The police were unable to **elicit** a confession from their primary suspect.

illicit (adj)—improper, in the sense of not being sanctioned by custom; not legal; unlawful; unlicensed

Example: **Illicit** drug trafficking along our borders has long been a serious problem.

Write two complete sentences, one using **elicit** and one using **illicit.**

82

elicit, illicit

Recall that the verb **elicit** means to draw forth, and the adjective **illicit** means improper. It may help to remember that **illicit** starts with the same three letters as *illegal*. If you're looking for the word that means illegal, or unlawful, then **illicit** is the correct choice.

Circle the proper word to make the sentence correct.

1. A good teacher always tries to (elicit, illicit) thought-provoking questions from students.

2. His (elicit, illicit) attempts at questioning Eva with no parent present led to his dismissal.

3. Ms. Murakami's homework assignment (elicited, illicited) protests from her math students.

4. Many oppose casino gambling because they think it leads to other (elicit, illicit) activities.

83

eminent, imminent

eminent (adj)—distinguished in reputation; towering above others in fame and accomplishment; standing out

Example: The **eminent** poet Robert Frost read a poem at President John F. Kennedy's inauguration.

imminent (adj)—impending; about to happen or occur

Example: The clouds on the horizon signaled an **imminent** storm.

Write one complete sentence containing both **eminent** and **imminent.**

84

eminent, imminent

It may help to remember that **eminent** begins with the same two letters as *emperor*, a ruler who is above others in position. **Imminent** begins with the same two letters as *impending*, which is its meaning.

Circle the correct words in the following paragraph.

In the novel *Flowers for Algernon*, the (eminent, imminent) Dr. Strauss gives his opinion that the (eminent, imminent) surgery on Charlie's brain might not produce immediate, safe results. However, Professor Nemur, an (eminent, imminent) psychologist, notes that there could be no (eminent, imminent) dangers. After all, they have practiced on mice and rats, the most (eminent, imminent) being the mouse Algernon. The truth is that Professor Nemur wants to present his findings to some doctors in Chicago, a group of (eminent, imminent) psychiatrists. Although he disagrees at first, Dr. Strauss eventually gives his approval to move ahead with the surgery. Both of these (eminent, imminent) doctors later regret that decision.

85

envelop, envelope

envelop (v)—to surround; to enclose with a covering

Example: The tree's seeds were **enveloped** with a hard shell to protect them from harm.

Example: A tall fence **envelops** the picnic area of the park.

envelope (n)—a container for a letter or similar object

Example: You will need a large **envelope** to mail all those pages.

Circle the proper word to make the sentence correct.

86

1. Greg used a wet sponge rather than licking so many (envelops, envelopes).

2. In the early morning hours, a thick fog sometimes (envelops, envelopes) the beach.

3. Victoria used a very large tarp to (envelop, envelope) her boat for the winter.

4. Manuel needed one hundred (envelops, envelopes) for the large mailing.

evoke, invoke

evoke (vb)—to call up or produce memories, feelings, and so forth; to elicit or draw forth; to call up

> Example: Revisiting her old elementary school **evoked** fond memories for Elisa.

invoke (vb)—to call for with earnest desire; to make supplication or to pray for; to call upon a deity; to declare to be binding or in effect; to petition or call for help

> Example: Peter **invoked** his right not to testify, citing the Fifth Amendment.

Write two complete sentences, one using **evoke** and one using **invoke.**

Which meaning of **invoke** did you use, and why did you use it?

87

evoke, invoke

Recall that the verb **evoke** means to call up or elict. The verb **invoke** means to pray for, to declare in effect, or to petition. It may help to remember that **evoke** begins with the same letter as *elicit*, its meaning.

Circle the proper word to make the sentence correct.

1. Their wedding album (evoked, invoked) fond memories for David and Sarah.

2. For Kate, singing "The Star-Spangled Banner" (evoked, invoked) strong emotions.

3. Visiting the Vietnam Veterans Memorial (evokes, invokes) many memories for veterans of that war.

4. Eli (evoked, invoked) the assistance of the entire team in fund-raising for the Red Cross.

5. (Evoking, Invoking) testimony from the hostile witness was an exercise in futility.

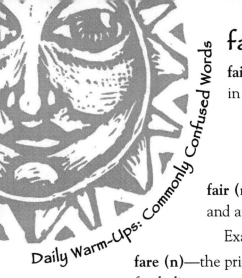

fair, fare

fair (adj)—free from bias, dishonesty, or injustice; moderately large; in meteorology, bright, sunny; free from blemish or imperfection

> Example: Mr. Riley had a reputation for being a very **fair** teacher.

> Example: **Fair** weather conditions allowed the space launch to proceed on schedule.

fair (n)—an exhibition, usually competitive, often with entertainment and amusements

> Example: State **fairs** are very popular and common in the Midwest.

fare (n)—the price of conveyance or passage on a bus, train, plane or other vehicles; food; diet

> Example: The **fares** for air travel have recently escalated.

> Example: The **fare** for the banquet was soup, salad, roasted chicken, and dessert.

fare (v)—to experience good or bad fortune or treatment

> Example: Cleo did not **fare** well in her attempt to get the ruling reversed.

Write two complete sentences, one using either the adjective or noun form of **fair** and one using either the noun or verb form of **fare.**

Review

Circle the proper word to make the sentence correct.

1. I must (complement, compliment) the chef on the tasty (desert, dessert).

2. It didn't bother her (conscience, conscious), because she was not (conscience, conscious) that her actions were (elicit, illicit).

3. I am (confidant, confident) that the two boys will help (each other, one another) with the project.

4. Please pay the (fair, fare) before you board the bus.

5. It (doesn't, don't) matter that Brian is (different from, different than) you.

6. There was so much (decent, descent, dissent) among the members of the (consul, council, counsel) that a decision could not be made.

7. Danielle knew she had broken the rules and prepared for the (eminent, imminent) punishment.

8. I will (device, devise) a plan to finish my paper before it is (dew, do, due).

90

farther, further

farther (adv)—at or to a greater distance (used to refer to measurable distance)

> Example: Texas is **farther** west than is Louisiana.

> Example: I walk **farther** to work than I do to the ballpark for Sunday's softball games.

further (adj or adv)—greater in time, degree, or extent; additionally

> Example: Frankly, I have no **further** interest in arguing with you over such trivia.

> Example: The **further** you go in the study of psychology, the more fascinating it becomes.

Write two complete sentences, one using the adverb **farther** and the other using either the adjective or adverb form of **further.**

Which sentence was easier to write? Why?

91

© 2003 J. Weston Walch, Publisher

farther, further

Remember that **farther** refers to distance, while **further** refers to time, degree, or extent. It may help to recall that the first three letters of **farther** spell *far*, a term usually used to describe a physical distance.

Circle the proper word to make the sentence correct.

1. The company has suspended (farther, further) negotiations for the contract.

2. The evidence was extensive and offered (farther, further) proof of the defendant's guilt.

3. I rode my bicycle (farther, further) down the road than Maggie did.

4. Hawaii is (farther, further) away than is Alaska.

5. There is no question we need (farther, further) review to be ready for the exam.

92

fewer, less

fewer (adj)—a smaller number (refers to things that can be counted)

   Example: There are **fewer** people smoking cigarettes today than there were ten years ago.

less (adj)—smaller in size, amount, or degree; not so large, great, or much (refers to things that cannot be counted)

   Example: There is **less** violence in the city than there was last year.

Write four complete sentences. Two sentences should contain **fewer,** and the other two should contain **less.**

93

fewer, less

Remember that **fewer** refers to things that can be counted, while **less** refers to a quantity that cannot be counted.

Circle the proper word to make the sentence correct.

1. There are (fewer, less) jellybeans in that jar than there were this morning.

2. I see that there is (fewer, less) milk in your glass than in mine.

3. There are (fewer, less) people looking for work because there are more jobs available.

4. (Fewer, Less) errors would occur in your lab work if you recorded the data precisely.

5. My car runs efficiently on (fewer, less) gasoline than yours does.

6. Gloria made (fewer, less) direct references to her reading than Marjorie did.

94

flair, flare

flair (n)—a natural talent or aptitude; instinctive discernment

Example: Monique has a **flair** for singing that is unequalled among her peers.

flare (v)—to burn in the wind with an unusually swaying flame, as a torch or a candle; to blaze; to burst out in sudden activity

Example: The cigarette lighter **flared** suddenly and singed Dawn's hair.

flare (n)—a bright blaze of fire or light; a device used to produce a sudden flame or fire

Example: The lost boys were fortunate to have two **flares** to signal their location.

Circle the proper word to make the sentence correct.

1. Jasmine's (flair, flare) for art won her a college scholarship to study design.
2. The two (flairs, flares) burned out before the rescuers were able to reach the lost hikers.
3. The (flair, flare) of the bonfire was seen five miles away.
4. The epidemic (flaired, flared) up and spread through the village.

95

© 2003 J. Weston Walch, Publisher

formally, formerly

formally (adv)—in a formal manner; conventional

Example: Ella and Craig were **formally** introduced for the first time at the dance.

formerly (adv)—previously or at an earlier time

Example: Diane Belcher was **formerly** known as Diane Forsberg.

Think of a memory trick or device that you can use to help you remember the meanings of **formally** and **formerly.** Then write a short paragraph that contains both **formally** and **formerly.**

96

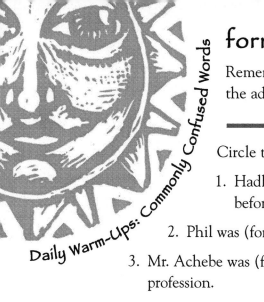

formally, formerly

Remember that the adverb **formally** means in a formal manner, while the adverb **formerly** means previously.

Circle the proper word to make the sentence correct.

1. Hadley had (formally, formerly) been a member of the Elks Club before he moved.

2. Phil was (formally, formerly) known as Mr. Philip Johnson.

3. Mr. Achebe was (formally, formerly) an engineer, and then he entered the law profession.

4. To the relief of the human-rights agency, the prisoners were (formally, formerly) treated according to the Geneva Conventions.

5. (Formally, Formerly), members of the Catholic church could not eat meat on Fridays.

97

© 2003 J. Weston Walch, Publisher

forth, fourth

forth (adv)—forward, onward, out into view

Example: The debaters put **forth** their best arguments in their closing remarks.

fourth (adj)—the number four used in a series

Example: Richard was the **fourth** of seven children.

Write a short paragraph using both **forth** and **fourth.**

98

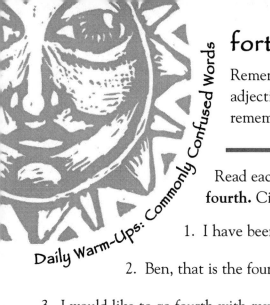

forth, fourth

Remember that **forth** is an adverb that means forward. **Fourth** is an adjective describing the number four used in a series. It may help to remember that **fourth** contains the word *four*.

Read each sentence below. Correct each mistake involving **forth** and **fourth.** Circle the incorrect word and write the correct word above it.

1. I have been friends with Anya since the forth grade.

2. Ben, that is the fourth banana you've eaten today!

3. I would like to go fourth with my plans to buy a car.

4. From this day forth, students at this school will wear uniforms.

5. This is the fourth time I've tried to go fourth with this project.

99

good, well

good (adj)—favorable or agreeable; virtuous or kind

Example: We enjoyed the show and had a **good** time at the theater.

Example: Nabil is a **good** person; he often volunteers his time at the local hospital.

well (adv)—in a proper manner

Example: She dances so **well,** I can't believe she never had lessons.

well (adj)—healthy

Example: I saw my grandfather yesterday; he's feeling **well.**

100

Write a short paragraph using the adjective **good** and the adverb and adjective forms of **well.** Circle each vocabulary word, and write the correct part of speech above it.

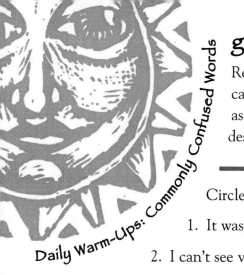

good, well

Recall that **good** is an adjective that means favorable or kind. **Well** can be used as an adjective to mean healthy, but it is most often used as an adverb to mean in a proper manner. Remember, if you are describing an activity, use the adverb **well.**

Circle the proper word to make the sentence correct.

1. It was (good, well) to see you yesterday at the basketball game.

2. I can't see very (good, well) at night, so I don't usually drive in the dark.

3. I felt (good, well) until I came down with a sore throat last week.

4. It was (good, well) of you to make that donation to the library.

5. Ruben is doing (good, well) in his calculus class because he completes all his homework.

101

grate, great

grate (n)—a framework of parallel or crossed bars over an opening; a metal framework to hold burning fuel, usually wood or coal

Example: Skipping from one **grate** to another along the sidewalk is a child's game.

grate (v)—to shred or pulverize by rubbing; to make or cause to make a rasping sound; to irritate

Example: Beth has jaw pain because she **grates** her teeth while she sleeps.

great (adj)—extremely large; notably big; remarkable; outstanding; eminent; distinguished; first rate; good

Example: Alex and Steve walked along the **Great** Wall during their visit to China.

102

Write three complete sentences, one using the noun **grate,** one using the verb **grate,** and one using the adjective **great.**

Which sentence was easiest for you to write? Why?

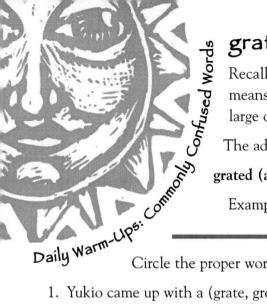

grate, great

Recall that the noun **grate** means a metal framework; the verb **grate** means to shred or to irritate; and the adjective **great** means extremely large or very good.

The adjective form of the verb **grate** is **grated.**

grated (adj)—pulverized; irritated; shredded

Example: The recipe called for **grated** carrots and onions.

Circle the proper word to make the sentence correct.

1. Yukio came up with a (grate, great) way to make extra spending money.

2. Ross reached (grate, great) heights when he pole vaulted over the seven-foot barrier.

3. Sara has a habit of (grating, greating) on the nerves of her closest friends.

4. The (grate, great) covering the area around the water drain was completely clogged.

5. Please add the (grated, greated) cheese to the pasta.

103

hang, hanged, hung

hang (vb)—to fasten above with no support from below; to suspend; to attach to a wall; to suspend by the neck until dead

Hang has two past forms and two *different* past participle forms, **hang, hanged, hung** and **hang, hung, hung. Hanged** is used exclusively in the sense of causing death. Therefore, do not use **hung** when referring to capital punishment or suicide.

Example: The four pictures were **hung** along the stairway leading to the balcony.

Example: Patrice **hung** the mirror on the back of the closet door.

Example: In some states, prisoners are **hanged** for capital offenses.

Example: The guards discovered that the inmate had **hanged** himself.

Write one complete sentence of your own, using either **hanged** or **hung.**

104

hang, hanged, hung

Recall that **hang** has two past forms and two different past participle forms; **hung** is used in most cases, while **hanged** is used only in the sense of causing death.

Circle the correct words in the following paragraph.

The prisoner was scheduled to be (hanged, hung) at dawn. Just before dawn, the warden received an important call from the prisoner's lawyer. He told the warden that Judge Clements was trying to stop the inmate from being (hanged, hung). Before he (hanged, hung) up, the lawyer told the warden to expect a call from the governor. The warden (hanged, hung) his badge on his shirt and proceeded to the gallows area to wait. The prisoner, head (hanged, hung) low, entered. Suddenly, the phone rang. After the warden (hanged, hung) up, he announced a stay of execution had been granted. The prisoner would not be (hanged, hung).

105

have, of

Have is a verb. When you say *could have, would have, might have, should have,* or the contractions *could've, would've, might've,* or *should've,* be sure you do not use the word **of** to mean **have.**

Example: I could **have** (not **of**) forgotten the tickets, but I didn't.

Example: I could**'ve** (not **of**) forgotten the tickets, but I didn't. (*Could've* is a contraction for *could have.*)

Of is a preposition and may never be used as a verb. It always begins a prepositional phrase that ends with a noun or a pronoun.

Example: I can't think **of** an idea without your help!

Example: There were several mistakes **of** a serious nature.

Write two sentences, one using **of** and the other using **could've.**

have, of

Remember that **have** is a verb. **Of** is a preposition and should not be used as a verb.

Read each sentence below. Correct each mistake involving **have** and **of.** Circle the incorrect word, and write the correct word above it.

1. There is no question that I could of won that race!

2. When I think of what might've been, I get angry with myself for not trying.

3. I would have entered the science fair if I could of thought of a project.

4. I should of known you were always a truthful person.

5. I could've graduated early, but I decided to stay for second semester.

6. I never would of thought that you would say such a thing.

107

hear, here

hear (vb)—to perceive by the ear; to learn by the ear or by being told; to be informed; to listen to; to give or pay attention to

Example: Despite all that noise, I can **hear** you clearly.

here (adv)—in this place; at this point

Example: **Here** are three things I want you to do before you go to work today.

Example: Please bring that chair over **here** next to the fireplace.

Write a short paragraph, using both **hear** and **here.** Exchange your paragraph with a classmate, and check each other's work.

108

hear, here

Recall that **hear** means to perceive by ear, while **here** means in this place or at this point. It may help to remember that the last three letters of **hear** spell *ear*.

Circle the proper word to make the sentence correct.

1. How can I help but (hear, here) you when you're yelling?

2. I am listening carefully, but I do not (hear, here) good reasons for overturning the verdict.

3. I want you to stand over (hear, here) by the monument while I take your picture.

4. (Hear, Here) clearly that I am not telling you to give up learning to write well.

5. Please list (hear, here) the things you want to improve through hard work and effort.

6. With his earplugs in, Bernie could not (hear, here) his neighbor's loud music.

109

© 2003 J. Weston Walch, Publisher

hoard, horde

hoard (n)—a supply or an accumulation that is hidden or carefully guarded for preservation or for future use

> Example: The settlers kept their **hoard** of food for winter in underground dugouts.

hoard (vb)—to accumulate in a hidden or carefully guarded place for future use

> Example: Ally **hoarded** the candy and refused to share it with her brother.

horde (n)—a large group, multitude, or number; a mass or a crowd; a tribe or a troop of nomads; a moving pack or swarm of animals

> Example: The horde of fans rushed the field after the home team won the game.

110

Write two complete sentences, one using the noun **horde** and one using either the noun or verb form of **hoard.**

hoard, horde

Recall that the noun **hoard** means a supply preserved for future use; the verb **hoard** means to accumulate for future use; and the noun **horde** means a large group.

Read each sentence below. Correct each mistake involving **horde** and **hoard.** Circle the incorrect word, and write the correct word above it.

1. The hoard of wild horses came thundering through the pass.

2. Nomads horded food by storing it in packs carried by their horses.

3. The hoard of weapons accumulated by the rebels was huge.

4. Do not horde all of the ice cream; save some for me.

5. Jesse and Alison feared the horde of wild buffalo stampeding toward them.

111

© 2003 J. Weston Walch, Publisher

hole, whole

hole (n)—an opening through something; a hollow place in a solid body or mass; an embarrassing position or predicament; a fault or a flaw

Example: The **hole** in Billy's shoes allowed his socks to become soiled.

hole (vb)—to make a hole or holes in; to put or drive into a hole; to bore; to pit; to hollow

Example: Larry **holed** his putt and let his partner try for the birdie.

whole (adj)—comprising the full quantity, amount, extent, or number; entire; full; total; undiminished; complete

Example: Always look at the **whole** picture before you make a decision.

Write a sentence that contains both the noun **hole** and the adjective **whole.**

112

hole, whole

Remember that **hole** as a noun is an opening or a gap; **hole** as a verb means to make a hole in; and **whole** as an adjective means complete. **Whole** can also be used as a noun.

whole (n)—a complete amount

Example: The **whole** is greater than its parts.

Circle the proper word to make the sentence correct.

1. I made a (hole, whole) in the outside screen in order to open the unlocked window.

2. I will (hole, whole) my tire again if I run over another nail.

3. Keisha drilled (holes, wholes) in the birdhouse just big enough for small birds.

4. Subtract 18 from the (hole, whole) to get the answer.

5. In her rebuttal, Rosario poked (holes, wholes) in her opponent's arguments.

6. The (hole, whole) outcome of the game was undecided until the final minute.

113

idle, idol

idle (adj)—not working; avoiding work; lazy; useless or groundless

Example: Too much **idle** time breeds boredom.

idle (vb)—to pass time without working; to move lazily; to run or cause to run at a slow speed or out of gear

Example: The car **idled** smoothly for ten minutes to warm it up in the freezing weather.

idol (n)—an image used as an object of worship or veneration; one who is adored

Example: Nomar Garciaparra is an **idol** for aspiring shortstops.

114

Write two sentences, one using the noun **idol** and one using either the adjective or verb form of **idle.**

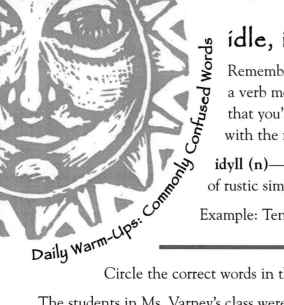

idle, idol, idyll

Remember that **idle** as an adjective means not working or lazy; **idle** as a verb means to move lazily; and an **idol** is one who is adored. Now that you're familiar with those words, remember not to confuse them with the noun **idyll.**

idyll (n)—a short poem about rustic (country) life; a scene or an event of rustic simplicity

Example: Tennyson's ***Idylls** of the King* is a classic in British literature.

Circle the correct words in the following paragraph.

The students in Ms. Varney's class were studying (idles, idols, idylls), many of which were written by her (idles, idols, idylls), the Romantic poets. The class had little time to remain (idle, idol, idyll), because there were so many poems to read. One (idle, idol, idyll) was particularly interesting. In it, an (idle, idol, idyll) mill worker falls in love with a fair maiden, an (idle, idol, idyll) in the town. To impress her, he writes an (idle, idol, idyll) comparing her to a warm summer's day where most (idled, idoled, idylled) away their time doing as little work as possible. However, his pleas for her hand fell on (idle, idol, idyll) ears.

115

imply, infer

imply (vb)—to signal or hint at a meaning

Example: I did not **imply** that I expected perfection.

Note: It is always the writer or the speaker who **implies** something.

infer (vb)—to deduce something from a hint or a signal

Example: I feel bad that you **inferred** from my comment that your artwork was poorly done.

Note: It is always the reader or listener who **infers.**

Think of a memory trick or device that you can use to help you remember the meanings of **imply** and **infer.** Then write a short paragraph containing both **imply** and **infer.**

116

imply, infer

Remember that the verb **imply** means to hint at something and always refers to the writer or speaker. The verb **infer** means to conclude or deduce and always refers to the reader or listener.

Circle the proper word to make the sentence correct.

1. From your reactions to my comments, I (imply, infer) you are angry.

2. Are you (implying, inferring) that Jane was responsible for the car accident?

3. The comments on your papers (imply, infer) that you should have done more research.

4. Juan (implied, inferred) that the referee's call had been unfair.

5. She did (imply, infer) from my comments that I was disappointed with her work.

6. You may (imply, infer) from all I've said that I have set high expectations for you.

117

its, it's

its (pronoun)—owned by; belonging to

Example: A horse uses **its** tail to swat flies and other insects.

it's—contraction of *it is*

Example: I don't want to go into any more detail about your birthday present; **it's** a secret.

Circle the proper word to make the sentence correct.

1. The camel stores water in (its, it's) body for weeks, requiring less fluid than most animals.

2. (Its, It's) clear that the answer to the problem is quite complex.

3. One can easily identify the lilac because of (its, it's) distinctive odor.

4. (Its, It's) interesting how the male pheasant shows off (its, it's) plumage by fanning (its, it's) tail feathers.

118

its, it's

Recall that the pronoun **its** shows ownership; **it's** is the contraction of *it is*. It may help to remember that if it makes sense to use the phrase *it is* in a situation, then it is correct to use the contraction **it's.**

Circle the proper word to make the sentence correct.

1. (Its, It's) never too late to apologize to Jordan for your oversight.

2. The company sent us a letter apologizing for (its, it's) mistake.

3. The furniture was worth only half of (its, it's) original value.

4. The lion cub had a difficult time reaching (its, it's) food.

Now write a short paragraph of your own using both the pronoun **its** and the contraction **it's.** Circle each vocabulary word, and write the correct part of speech above it.

119

Review

Circle the proper word to make the sentence correct.

1. (Its, It's) lucky that you are (hear, here) now, because the tickets are almost sold out.

2. Does your statement (imply, infer) that you want to discuss the situation (farther, further)?

3. Brooke (hanged, hung) the poster to cover a (hole, whole) in the wall.

4. This is the (forth, fourth) homework assignment you have forgotten at home.

5. Please don't (hoard, horde) the potato chips; I have (fewer, less) chips than you have!

6. My older sister is my (idle, idol, idyll) because she sings and dances so (good, well).

7. I would (have, of) helped you with your research if you had come to the library.

8. Mario did a (grate, great) job cooking dinner last night.

lay, lie

lay (vb)—to put; to place something

   Example: The baby **laid** his head down and immediately went to sleep.

  Note: The present, past, and past participles are *lay*, *laid*, and *laid*.

lie (vb)—to recline or remain in a reclining position

   Example: Linda has **lain** down for an afternoon nap every day of her long life.

   Example: Yesterday, Linda **lay** down for her afternoon nap, as usual.

  Note: The present, past, and past participles are *lie*, *lay*, and *lain*.

Circle the proper word to make the sentence correct.

1. It was precisely at four P.M. that Melanie (lay, laid) down for a rest.
2. The biggest valleys we know (lie, lay) at the bottom of high mountains.
3. I cannot (lie, lay) down for a rest until the lawn is mowed.
4. The rebels (lay, laid) down their arms and surrendered the day before yesterday.

121

lay, lie

Remember that **lay** means *to place*, and **lie** means *to recline*.

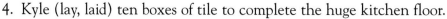

Circle the proper word to make the sentence correct.

1. Just (lie, lay) your tools on the workbench, and let me show you what needs to be done.

2. The wounded dog (lay, laid) there while the veterinarian examined and cleaned the cut.

3. According to legend, Rip Van Winkle had (lain, laid) down and slept for 100 years.

4. Kyle (lay, laid) ten boxes of tile to complete the huge kitchen floor.

Write four sentences using the same method as in the examples above, with a choice for the terms **lie** and **lay** or their other forms. Then exchange your sentences with a classmate's, and complete his or her sentences by circling the proper term to make the sentence correct.

122

lead, led

lead (vb)—(pronounced with a long *e*) to go before or first; to conduct or escort; to guide in a decision

> Example: Today, Mary **leads** the procession from the gym to the auditorium.

led (vb)—past tense of *to lead*

> Example: Jason **led** the band down Main Street for the Fourth of July parade.

Circle the proper word to make the sentence correct.

1. Elvira (lead, led) all competitors in the voting for class president.

2. I will (lead, led) you through the steps necessary to write a good research paper.

3. One mountain (lead, led) to another, making crossing the Rockies a daunting task.

4. The initial attack by the rebels (lead, led) to a full-blown battle to control the river.

Write four sentences of your own. Use the verb **lead** in two of them and the verb **led** in the two others.

123

lead, led

Lead can also be a noun with two different meanings and pronunciations.

lead (n)—(pronounced with a long *e*) a person who leads; a leash

Example: Jack put his horse on a **lead** to move it around the corral.

Example: Denzel Washington played the **lead** in the movie about the life of Malcolm X.

lead (n)—(pronounced with a short *e*) a heavy metal; graphite in a pencil

Example: I hope you don't get poisoned by the **lead** in your pencil.

124

Circle the proper word to make the sentence correct.

1. The amount of (lead, led) in the paint made it hazardous for young children.

2. Mrs. Royce will choose the (lead, led) for the role of Annie in *Annie Get Your Gun*.

3. In the early part of dog training, Aisha kept her German shepherd on a (lead, led).

4. The (lead, led) in Bonnie's pencil kept breaking during art class.

Write a paragraph using all the noun and verb forms of **lead** and the past tense form, **led.** Share your paragraph with a classmate to make sure all forms are used correctly.

literally, figuratively

literally (adv)—in an exact sense or manner; actually; virtually

> Example: Hannah took the remark **literally** and thought cats and dogs were falling from the sky.

figuratively (adv)—in an analogous sense

> Example: Hannah then took the remark **figuratively** and realized that it was just raining really hard.

Many people use the word **literally** when they really mean **figuratively.** The following paragraph contains misuses of **literally.** Identify the mistakes and correct them.

The phone literally rang 400 times last night. My grandmother called first. She told me how she literally waited in line at the grocery store for hours earlier that day. "The lines were literally a mile long," she said. Then Jen called from her cell phone. She said she was on the highway, literally driving 150 mph because she was late. She also said that she literally ran a hundred red lights before she got on the highway. She tends to exaggerate. Then my sister called asking for my mom. My mom was late picking her up at soccer practice. "I have literally been waiting all day," she said. I was literally on the phone all night.

125

literally, figuratively

People use **literally** so frequently that you can probably remember hearing it. Think of at least three times when you have heard someone say **literally** when he or she should have said **figuratively.** Perhaps you can even remember a time when you used the word incorrectly. If not, make up your own sentences in which **literally** is used incorrectly.

Now write two sentences in which **literally** is used correctly.

126

loose, lose

loose (adj)—free; not close together; not tied or bound to anything

Example: Gloria preferred wearing **loose** sweaters that hung below her waist.

lose (vb)—to suffer the loss of; to fail to keep, perceive, or maintain

Example: Paul did not **lose** his house key after all; it was in his jacket pocket.

Circle the correct words in the following paragraph.

James, who would rarely (loose, lose) his temper, was now furious. His best friend, Glen, who had a reputation for having a (loose, lose) mouth, bad-mouthed James for (loosing, losing) control of himself during the recent football game. The football had come (loose, lose) from the running back, and James, a defensive end, jumped on the (loose, lose) ball to recover the fumble. However, the referee claimed the runner was down by contact, and his team did not (loose, lose) the ball. James jumped up, took off his helmet, and began to let (loose, lose) at the official, who refrained from (loosing, losing) his composure. James's (loosing, losing) his temper cost his team a 15-yard penalty, and they ended up (loosing, losing) the game.

127

loose, lose

Let's review the words. **Loose** means free or untied. **Lose** means to misplace or fail to win. An easy way to remember how to use **lose** correctly is to recall that it is related to the word *lost*.

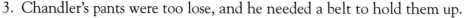

The following sentences may contain an incorrect form of **loose** or **lose.** Circle the misused word(s), and write the correct form(s) above. Some sentences may already be correct.

1. Joey losely tied Rachel's shoes so that she would trip and fall.

2. Monica was still upset about loosing her earrings.

3. Chandler's pants were too lose, and he needed a belt to hold them up.

4. Phoebe would lose her head if it weren't attached.

5. Ross felt like a looser because he couldn't get a date.

6. Every time Emma would loose her penguin, Rachel would know Joey had stolen it.

Now write two sentences of your own, making sure to use both **loose** and **lose.**

128

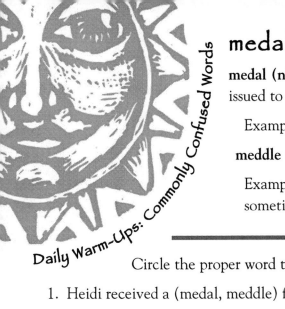

medal, meddle

medal (n)—a flat piece of metal bearing an inscription or a design, issued to commemorate a person, an action, or an event

Example: Claire won three gold **medals** at the state swim meet.

meddle (vb)—to intrude in the affairs of others; to interfere

Example: When you **meddle** into the affairs of others, you sometimes get hurt feelings.

Circle the proper word to make the sentence correct.

1. Heidi received a (medal, meddle) for her rescue of the small boy.

2. Percy was not one to (medal, meddle) into the personal business of his employees.

3. Jeff's apple pie took the gold (medal, meddle) at the county fair.

Write two of your own sentences just like the examples above with a choice of each word. Exchange your examples with a classmate's, and choose the correct words for his or her two sentences.

129

medal, meddle, mettle

Remember that a **medal** is a flat piece of metal awarded to a person. **Meddle** is a verb meaning *to interfere*. Be careful not to confuse these two words with the noun **mettle.**

mettle (n)—courage and fortitude; disposition of temperament

Example: Arpad showed his **mettle** when he moved into the enemy camp while wounded.

Circle the proper word to make the sentence correct.

1. I don't think anyone has won six gold (medals, meddles, mettles) in any one Olympics.

2. Whatever you do, remember not to (medal, meddle, mettle) with a successful program.

3. The (medal, meddle, mettle) of the troops was apparent when they came under enemy fire.

4. It was Candy, not Val, who (medaled, meddled, mettled) into Jennifer's affairs.

5. His true (medal, meddle, mettle) was never public because he was so humble and shy.

130

passed, past

passed (vb)—past tense of the verb *to pass*; to go by without stopping; to proceed; to undergo a test, a trial, or a course of study with favorable results; to approve as by a legislative body

Example: Allen illegally **passed** the school bus while its red lights were blinking.

Example: Janice **passed** every one of her exams with a B or better.

Example: The state legislators **passed** a law making drunk driving a felony.

past (n)—a time before now

Example: The **past** teaches us many lessons for the future.

Circle the proper word to make the sentence correct.

1. Carl had many secrets hidden in his shady (passed, past).

2. Chang-Rae (passed, past) his driver's test on his first try.

3. Jim (passed, past) "Go" playing Monopoly four times, and not once did he go to jail.

4. Players from the (passed, past) were on the field to honor Ted Williams.

131

passed, past

Let's quickly review. **Passed** means *went by*, and **past** means *a former time*.

Past can also be an adjective.

past (adj)—no longer current; having existed or occurred at an earlier time

> Example: Gary learned from his **past** mistakes, and he profited from those lessons.

Circle the proper word to make the sentence correct. Identify the part of speech of the word you circled, and write it at the end of the sentence.

1. Kyle's (passed, past) actions clouded his reputation and forced him to behave himself. _____

2. In the (passed, past), I have tried to overlook your rude comments, but I no longer can. _____

3. Having (passed, past) the entrance examination, Luke was accepted at the private school. _____

4. Josh was (passed, past) having his parents check to see if his homework was done. _____

132

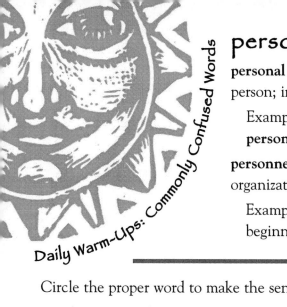

personal, personnel

personal (adj)—referring to characteristics pertaining to a particular person; individual; private; done in person

> Example: My reasons for not going to the party are purely **personal.**

personnel (n)—a group of employees; persons active in an organization

> Example: All **personnel** will receive a pay raise of five percent beginning immediately.

Circle the proper word to make the sentence correct.

1. The New England Patriots did not have the (personal, personnel) to win the championship this year.

2. Barry's remarks were so (personal, personnel) that Lauren was highly offended.

3. You may carry one bag of (personal, personnel) belongings on the plane with you.

4. The company had to lay off half of its (personal, personnel) in order to avoid bankruptcy.

133

personal, personnel

Write the definitions of **personal** and **personnel** in your own words. It will help you remember what they mean if you understand them in your own context.

Circle the proper word to make the sentence correct.

1. All (personal, personnel) must report to spring training by February 20.

2. His (personal, personnel) effects were put into a bag when he was arrested.

3. I need to warn all (personal, personnel) of the imminent dangers of asbestos.

4. My (personal, personnel) thoughts on the subject will remain private until tomorrow.

134

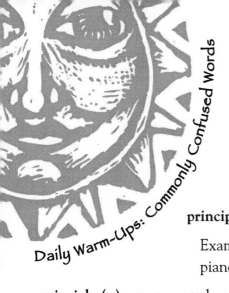

principal, principle

principal (n)—a head or a chief; the head director of a school; a person who takes the lead in any activity, as in a play; something of chief importance; a sum of money owed as a debt upon which interest is calculated

> Example: The high school **principal** was known for his high energy and fairness.

principal (adj)—first in rank, importance, or value

> Example: The **principal** reason why I chose to study guitar rather than piano is that the instrument is more portable.

principle (n)—an accepted or a professed rule of action or conduct; a fundamental, primary, or general law or truth from which others are derived; a fundamental doctrine or tenet

> Example: Learning the basic **principles** of algebra will help you in your study of science.

Write four sentences. Use **principal** in two and **principle** in two.

135

© 2003 J. Weston Walch, Publisher

principal, principle

To put it simply, as an adjective, **principal** means primary. As a noun, it can mean school administrator or sum of money. **Principle** means idea or doctrine.

You can use the following tricks to help you remember which word to use:

The princi<u>pal</u> is my <u>pal</u>.

The princi<u>ple</u> is a ru<u>le</u>.

Circle the correct words in the following paragraph.

The (principal, principle) of Podunk High School was reviewing the financial accounts of the various clubs in her school. She was concerned because she noticed a discrepancy in one account. While she had never studied the (principals, principles) of economics, she was smart enough to see errors, and her (principals, principles) could not let her overlook what she saw. She always believed that the (principals, principles) of honesty and integrity led to success, and the (principal, principle) reason she was a (principal, principle) was to lead, teach, and model those virtues. Upon further investigation, she realized that the interest earned by the club had never been calculated. Her first and (principal, principle) concern was that someone had meddled with the account.

136

quiet, quite

quiet (adj)—making no sound or noise; silent; peaceful; being at rest

Example: The **quiet** church was soon bustling with wedding guests.

quiet (n)—freedom from noise or unwanted sound; rest; repose; calm

Example: The wedding guests interrupted the **quiet** in the church.

quiet (vb)—to make quiet, tranquil, or peaceful; to pacify; to silence

Example: The minister came to the altar and soon **quieted** the wedding guests.

quite (adv)—wholly, completely, entirely; actually, really, or truly

Example: I am **quite** surprised that you did not do well on the test.

Circle the proper word to make the sentence correct. Identify the part of speech of the word you circled, and write it at the end of each sentence.

1. Remain (quiet, quite) until everyone has finished the test. _____

2. A tidal wave is huge and (quiet, quite) dangerous to coastal areas. _____

3. The (quiet, quite) was spooky as night fell in the desert. _____

4. I was taken (quiet, quite) seriously when I predicted the test would be (quiet, quite) hard. _____ _____

137

quiet, quite

To review, **quiet** is the opposite of *noisy*. **Quite** means *completely* or *entirely*. You have to pay special attention to spelling when writing these words. It is especially easy to mix up the letters when typing, and a spell-check program will recognize both of them as correct.

Circle the proper word to make the sentence correct.

1. By trapping the fox, the farmer (quieted, quited) down the chickens in the barnyard.

2. Briggs (quieted, quited) the crowd by raising his hands and asking for silence.

3. This winter has been (quiet, quite) cold, well below normal.

4. (Quiet, Quite) fell over the class in the hall as the professor began his lecture.

Write two sentences of your own, each containing both **quiet** and **quite.** Spell these words carefully; they are easily confused.

138

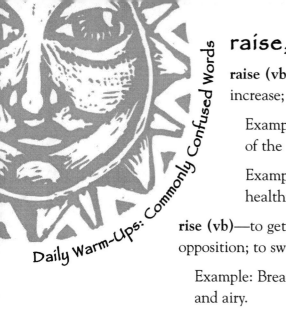

raise, rise

raise (vb)—to move something to a higher position; to elevate; to increase; to lift; to serve in the capacity of a parent

Example: Every morning the custodians **raise** the flag at the front of the school.

Example: Angelina and Bill were fine parents and **raised** five healthy children.

rise (vb)—to get up from a lying position; to go up; to rebel or revolt by opposition; to swell or puff up

Example: Bread dough must **rise** in order for the bread to be soft and airy.

Write four sentences. Use **raise** in two and **rise** in two.

139

raise, rise

Raise and **rise** are also nouns.

raise (n)—an increase in the amount of wages; the amount of that increase

Example: Benjamin gives his employees a decent **raise** every year.

rise (n)—an act or instance of rising

Example: The **rise** in gasoline prices this year has been dramatic.

Circle the proper word to make the sentence correct.

1. Please (raise, rise) for the flag salute.

2. To avoid everyone talking at once, please (raise, rise) your hand to be called upon.

3. Farmers in Maine are well known for (raising, rising) potatoes.

4. The (raise, rise) in temperatures caused the vegetable farmers some concern.

5. Sigmund and Hilda (raised, rised) llamas on their farm for a living.

6. The French pastry was left to (raise, rise) for one hour before baking.

Think of a trick to help you remember the meaning of these two words. Share your ideas with a classmate.

140

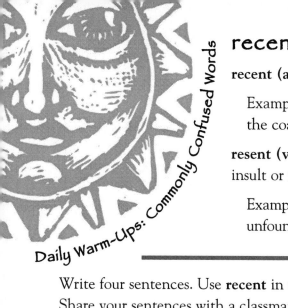

recent, resent

recent (adj)—having just happened; occurred lately

Example: The most **recent** snowstorm dumped two feet of snow on the coastal towns.

resent (vb)—to show displeasure or indignation at, as from a sense of insult or injury

Example: I **resent** your comments because they are completely unfounded in reality.

Write four sentences. Use **recent** in two of them and **resent** in the other two. Share your sentences with a classmate to make sure the words have been used correctly.

141

recent, resent

Remember, **recent** involves time. **Resent** is a verb, so it will always be some type of action. Think of your own trick to help you remember these two words. Since the only letters that differ are *c* and *s*, this difference will be a good place for you to start.

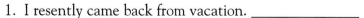

Find the mistakes in the following sentences. Cross out the incorrect word, and write the proper word in the space provided. If the sentence is correct as it is, write *correct* in the space provided.

1. I resently came back from vacation. _____

2. Ricky recents your resent remarks. _____ _____

3. I could tell that the photo was resent because Kate's hair was the same length. _____

4. She still resented every mean thing Ryan ever said to her. _____

5. I recently received a phone call from my uncle in Australia. _____

142

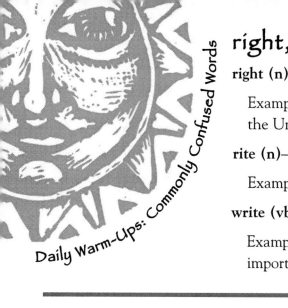

right, rite, write

right (n)—a just claim or title, legal, moral, or prescriptive

Example: Individual **rights** are protected under the Constitution of the United States.

rite (n)—a formal or ceremonial act or procedure

Example: The **rite** of marriage is often performed by a cleric.

write (vb)—to inscribe; to compose

Example: I **write** in my journal every day about those things important to me.

Write a paragraph using all of the words defined above. Share your paragraph with a classmate to make sure all the words have been used correctly.

143

right, rite, write

In addition to being a noun, **right** can also be an adjective, an adverb, and a verb.

right (adj)—in accordance with what is good, proper, or just; correct; located on or near the side that is turned toward the east when the subject is facing north

Example: Bert wanted to make a **right** turn and stay on the **right** side of the road.

right (adv)—in a straight or direct line; directly

Example: I want you to go **right** to the post office before you play baseball.

right (vb)—to restore to an upright position; to put in proper order or condition

Example: Most salespeople will work to **right** any mistakes they have made.

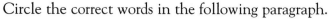

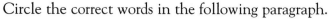

Circle the correct words in the following paragraph.

Dana is visiting the Casaba, an aboriginal tribe living (right, rite, write) in the middle of a huge forest in southern Australia. Every day he (rights, rites, writes) in his journal to get the (right, rite, write) perspective on all he witnesses. Today he (rights, rites, writes) about attending the (right, rite, write) of passage ceremony for the young boys, a (right, rite, write) few outsiders have ever seen. He records every step of the process and plans later to have the chief (right, rite, write) any wrong perceptions he has.

144

Daily Warm-Ups: Commonly Confused Words

© 2003 J. Weston Walch, Publisher

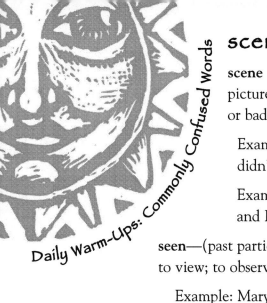

scene, seen

scene (n)—a place where some action or event occurs; any view or picture; an embarrassing outbreak or display of anger, strong feeling, or bad manners; a division of a play

Example: The child had a tantrum and created a **scene** when he didn't get his way.

Example: In the final **scene** of *Hamlet,* the king, the queen, Laertes, and Hamlet all die.

seen—(past participle of the verb *to see*) to perceive with the eyes; to look at; to view; to observe; to regard

Example: Mary had **seen** several ways to solve the math problem.

Note: Used as a verb, **seen** requires a helping verb.

Write three of your own sentences, using both **scene** and **seen** in each of them. Share your sentences with a classmate and discuss whether each of you used the words correctly.

145

scene, seen

It is easy to remember **seen.**

I can <u>see</u> what can be <u>seen</u>.

If you use **seen** in a sentence and it does not mean some form of *to see*, then you probably need to use **scene.**

Circle the proper word to make the sentence correct.

1. The (scene, seen) was one of rustic beauty, with the forest as a background.

2. (Scene, Seen) as a solution to a complex problem, the ordinance was passed by the council.

3. Stan, blindsided, had never (scene, seen) the punch coming.

4. In the second act of the play, there is a hilarious (scene, seen).

5. Please do not make a (scene, seen) over the error made by the store clerk.

6. Lenny had not (scene, seen) the butterfly in its cocoon stage.

146

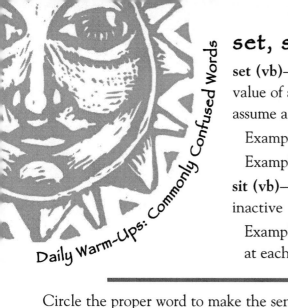

set, sit

set (vb)—to put something from one place to another; to fix the value of at a certain amount or rate; to pass below the horizon; to assume a rigid state

Example: Phyllis **set** the dish on the table and left the room.

Example: The sun rises in the east and **sets** in the west.

sit (vb)—to be seated; to be located or situated; to remain quiet or inactive

Example: Please **sit** at the table according to the name cards placed at each seat.

Circle the proper word to make the sentence correct.

1. Vera (set, sit) the lamp on the table nearest the French doors.
2. Belinda and Lily (set, sat) patiently, waiting for the secretary to call their names.
3. Once you (set, sit) down, we can begin the class.
4. (Set, Sit) the plant nearer to the window so it will get some natural light.
5. Carl (set, sit) his alarm clock before he went to sleep.
6. If you look carefully, you will see that the valuable sculpture (sets, sits) near the wall.

147

set, sit

Set can also be a noun.

set (n)—collection of articles designed for use together; a member, group, or combination of things similar in nature, design, or function

Example: Lavina's antique **set** of sterling silver dinnerware was very valuable.

To review, **sit** means to put the body in a seated position. **Set** as a verb means *to place*, and **set** as a noun means *a collection*.

Write a paragraph using **sit** and **set** as a verb and as a noun. Exchange your paragraph with a classmate's, and identify in his or her paragraph the parts of speech for each instance of **set** or **sit.**

148

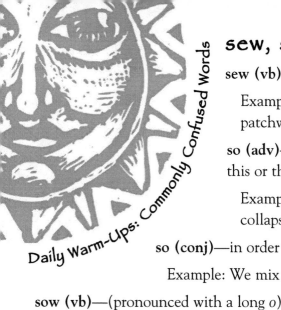

sew, so, sow

sew (vb)—to join or attach by stitches; to make or repair by sewing

> Example: Annmarie **sewed** together old pieces of cloth for a patchwork quilt.

so (adv)—in the way or manner indicated, described, or implied; in this or that manner or fashion; thus; very, extremely

> Example: You can only construct a building **so** high before it could collapse.

so (conj)—in order that; with the result that

> Example: We mix those chemicals **so** we can get a chemical reaction.

sow (vb)—(pronounced with a long *o*) to plant

Example: You need to **sow** the seed for your vegetables after the last frost.

sow (n)—(pronounced with a short *o*) a female pig

Example: The large **sow** gave birth to seven piglets.

Write five sentences of your own, each containing one of the words above.

149

© 2003 J. Weston Walch, Publisher

Review

Circle the proper word to make the sentence correct.

1. If you don't put your wallet in your pocket, you could (loose, lose) it.

2. Daryl had (laid, lain) in the hospital for a month before he came out of a deep coma.

3. Just (set, sit) on that chair until I finish with this customer.

4. The interest he pays monthly on his loan exceeds his payment on the (principal, principle).

5. The police car (passed, past) by with its lights flashing.

6. You have the (right, rite, write) to an attorney.

7. The couple's fight was (quiet, quite) a (scene, seen).

8. The hostess (lead, led) us to our table at the restaurant.

150

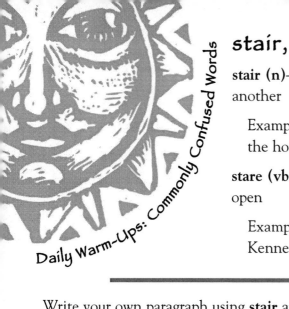

stair, stare

stair (n)—one of a flight or series of steps going from one level to another

> Example: Edward built a new set of **stairs** for the back entrance to the house.

stare (vb)—to gaze fixedly and intently, especially with the eyes wide open

> Example: Upset by his rude remark, Blake **stared** angrily at Kenneth.

Write your own paragraph using **stair** and **stare** incorrectly. Then give your paragraph to a classmate for him or her to correct. Check to make sure your classmate found all your misuses.

151

stair, stare

Stare can be a noun as well as a verb.

stare (n)—a fixed look with the eyes wide open

Example: Emily tried to avoid Blake's **stare** but was unable to do so.

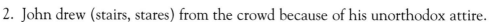

Circle the proper word to make the sentence correct.

1. Sydney had to climb seven flights of (stairs, stares) to reach her apartment.

2. John drew (stairs, stares) from the crowd because of his unorthodox attire.

3. Holly (staired, stared) at the calculus test with a blank mind.

4. Start at the bottom, and climb the (stairs, stares) to reach your dreams.

5. Joseph was completely unabashed by the (stairs, stares) of his audience.

Write two sentences. Use **stair** in one and **stare** as a noun in the other.

152

stationary, stationery

stationary (adj)—not moving; standing still; having a fixed position

Example: The stage in the auditorium is **stationary** and cannot be moved.

stationery (n)—writing paper

Example: Kara uses perfumed **stationery** when she writes letters to her friends.

Circle the proper word to make the sentence correct.

1. The huge machine was bolted to the floor to keep it (stationary, stationery).

2. Remain (stationary, stationery) while the others dance around you.

3. Please do not use lined (stationary, stationery) when writing formal letters.

4. Loretta bought several boxes of fancy (stationary, stationery) to give as presents.

5. Use high quality, white, 8½" × 11" (stationary, stationery) when writing business letters.

6. To keep the posts (stationary, stationery), they were placed in concrete.

153

© 2003 J. Weston Walch, Publisher

stationary, stationery

Remember, **stationary** means *not movable*. **Stationery** is the *paper* you use on which to write letters. The difference between these two words, the *a* and the *e*, is so small that you may not have even known there was a difference until now. It may be helpful to remember that station<u>a</u>ry is an <u>a</u>djective that describes when something is not movable. Station<u>e</u>ry is used less and less every day because of <u>e</u>-mail. Instead of writing letters to your friends, you probably keep in touch more using e-mail.

The tricks above may not be helpful to you. You may be able to think of a better way for you to remember the meaning of these words. Think of at least two more ways to remember the difference between the two words. Then share your ideas with a classmate.

154

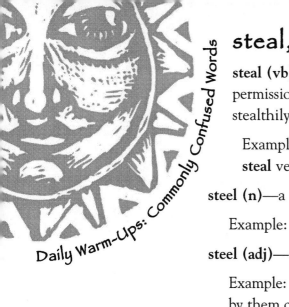

steal, steel

steal (vb)—to take the property of another or others without permission; to commit or practice theft; to move, happen, or elapse stealthily or unobtrusively

Example: Raccoons love unprotected gardens from which they can **steal** vegetables.

steel (n)—a modified form of iron; a hard metal made from modified iron

Example: My kitchen sink is made of stainless **steel.**

steel (adj)—a quality suggestive of steel

Example: Patrick had **steel** principles, and he stuck by them consistently.

Write three sentences. Use **steal** in one, **steel** as a noun in one, and **steel** as an adjective in the last.

155

steal, steel

Remember, **steal** means to take something without permission. **Steel** is a metal.

Circle the proper word to make the sentence correct.

1. Courtney's nerves of (steal, steel) made her a daunting opponent in debate.

2. Bailey was concerned that Steve would (steal, steel) the scene from her onstage.

3. Let's (steal, steel) a few minutes away from this place and relax.

4. Mark would (steal, steel) your shirt off your back if he could.

5. The (steal, steel) bars covered the windows of the jewelry store to discourage thieves from (stealing, steeling).

6. The vault, made of solid (steal, steel), was the latest addition to the store.

156

than, then

than (conj)—used for comparisons; used to introduce the second element or clause of a comparison of inequality

Example: You are far more intelligent **than** you think.

then (adv)—at that time in the past; next in time, order, or space; at another time in the future; in that case; in addition; besides; yet; on the other hand

Example: Let's go to the movies and **then** go out to eat.

Circle the proper word to make the sentence correct.

1. That building seems taller (than, then) this one.

2. I don't see how you can say one thing and (than, then) change your mind so easily.

3. There is no question that lead is heavier (than, then) silver.

4. Buildings made of steel are much stronger (than, then) those made of wood.

5. I like to get Chinese food every now and (than, then).

157

© 2003 J. Weston Walch, Publisher

than, then

Let's review. **Than** is used in a comparison, and **then** tells *when*. **Then** is easy to remember because it rhymes with *when*.

Write a paragraph using **than** and **then** at least five times each. Use each word incorrectly once or twice in your paragraph. Give your paragraph to a classmate to read and correct any mistakes. Then when your paper is returned, make sure he or she found all the mistakes.

158

their, there, they're

their (pronoun)—the possessive case of the pronoun *they*, indicating ownership; usually used as an adjective

Example: Grant and Hunter gave **their** best performance on the second night of the play.

there (adv)—of or at a place; to, into, or toward a place

Example: **There** are several reasons why I don't want to dance.

Example: Over **there** is the door the president will walk through.

they're—contraction of *they are*

Example: **They're** supposed to give you the answer before we proceed with the project.

Write six sentences. Use each word in two sentences. Then exchange your sentences with a classmate, and read his or hers to make sure the words are used correctly.

159

their, there, they're

These three words are often misused because they all sound the same. By remembering simple tricks, it is easy to use the correct word. When using **their,** make sure the word shows ownership. <u>There</u> can easily be remembered by <u>here</u>. **There** refers to a place or location, just as *here* does. **They're** is a contraction for *they are*. When you use **they're,** ask yourself if the words *they are* fit in the same spot.

Circle the correct words in the following paragraph.

People can be very funny, by which I mean strange and weird, not humorous. Take those who think (their, there, they're) ideas are the only ones that matter. I think (their, there, they're) suffering from delusions of grandeur. Then (their, there, they're) are those who want to force (their, there, they're) ideas on you, even though you make it clear that you do not share (their, there, they're) position. However, (their, there, they're) is no limit to (their, there, they're) boldness. Often (their, there, they're) so rude that (their, there, they're) still talking at you even after you've said you're not interested.

to, too, two

to (prep)—movement toward; in a direction toward; toward or reaching the state of

> Example: Darren went through the hall, into the room, and up **to** the front.

> Example: Please take this letter **to** the post office and mail it.

too (adv)—in addition; also; more than sufficient; excessively

> Example: Marich and Meghan wanted to go to the circus, **too.**

> Example: Rheatha used **too** much butter in the cake recipe.

two (n, adj, pronoun)—the number 2; equal to one plus one; having two parts

> Example: I have told you **two** times that a negative times a negative equals a positive.

> Example: The **two** of you are going to work together.

People confuse these words every day because they all sound the same. Take a document that you have already written, whether it is a rough draft or a final draft. It can be an essay, a report, or a piece of creative writing. Look through the text, lightly circling in pencil **to, too,** and **two.** Using the definitions above as a reference, make sure you have used the correct form. If it is incorrect, write in the correct word.

161

© 2003 J. Weston Walch, Publisher

to, too, two

To means the same as *toward*. If you can replace **to** with *toward*, then you most likely have used it correctly. **Too** means *very* or *also*. Replace **too** with either of these words to make sure you have used it correctly. You should be able to replace **two** with the number 2.

Circle the correct words in the following paragraph.

Often there are (to, too, two) many people (to, too, two) tell a secret. Any more than (to, too, two) poses a serious threat that the secret will be revealed. (To, Too, Two) often we make the mistake of trusting (to, too, two) many people, and we hear the secret coming back to us from (to, too, two) different sources. It is like walking into a stone wall, because the shock is almost (to, too, two) much to bear. The (to, too, two) lessons (to, too, two) be learned are that more than (to, too, two) people can't keep a secret, so tell it only (to, too, two) the one person you trust most.

162

vice, vise

vice (n)—an immoral or evil habit or practice; immoral conduct; degrading or depraved behavior; a fault, a defect, or a shortcoming

Example: Barry Goldwater once said that extremism in the defense of liberty is no **vice.**

vise (n)—a device usually having two jaws that may be brought together or separated by means of a screw, a lever, or the like, used to hold an object firmly in place

Example: To be sure the board you are cutting is stationary, put it in a **vise.**

Circle the proper word to make the sentence correct.

1. Many consider gambling to be a serious (vice, vise).
2. The (vice, vise) of greed often takes over reason and common sense in our actions.
3. Caught in the (vice, vise) of Al's firm grip, Bill was unable to move to his left.
4. We have enough (vices, vises) to keep us busy trying to protect our reputations.
5. Pride is a (vice, vise) that more often than not gets us into trouble.

Write two sentences of your own. Use **vice** in one and **vise** in the other.

163

vice, vise

Remember, **vice** is a bad habit or fault. A **vise** is a device that holds something in place. It may help you to remember that the wrong use of **vise** is in de<u>vice</u>.

Now think of another trick to help you remember the meanings of **vice** and **vise.** Share your ideas with a classmate. It may be helpful to remember what **vice** means if you have examples and relate them to yourself. What are some of your vices? Think of as many examples as you can.

164

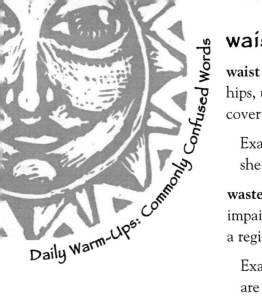

waist, waste

waist (n)—the part of the body in humans between the ribs and the hips, usually the narrowest part of the torso; the part of a garment covering this part of the body; midsection

Example: The trainer insisted that Delta bend at the **waist** when she touched her toes.

waste (n)—useless consumption; neglect; gradual destruction, impairment, or decay; devastation or ruin, as from war or fire; a region or place devastated or ruined

Example: Americans accumulate so much **waste** that our landfills are almost full.

Write a paragraph using **waist** and **waste** at least twice each. Then share your paragraph with a classmate to make sure the words are used correctly.

165

waist, waste

Waste can also be a verb or an adjective.

waste (v)—to consume, spend, or employ uselessly; to use to no profit; to wear away; to destroy or consume gradually; to ruin

    Example: The runner **wasted** precious energy trying to take the lead before he was ready.

waste (adj)—not used or in use; rejected as useless or worthless

    Example: **Waste** materials from nuclear power plants pose problems for the environment.

Circle the proper word to make the sentence correct. After you select the correct word for each sentence, identify the part of speech of that word, and write it on the line.

1. Because of the drought, the lettuce crop (waisted, wasted) away and was destroyed. _____

2. It is a (waist, waste) of my time trying to help you when you don't help yourself. _____

3. Evan's girth had grown so great that he measured 40 inches at the (waist, waste). _____

4. (Waist, Waste) products from aerosol cans damage the ozone layer. _____

5. The (waist, waste) generated by my family is excessive. _____

166

waive, wave

waive (vb)—to refrain from claiming or insisting on; to forgo; to defer; to postpone

> Example: Steve **waived** his right to an appeal when he accepted a plea bargain.

wave (vb)—to move gently back and forth or up and down; to cause to flutter or to have wavelike motion; to signal or make a signal by waving

> Example: The passengers **waved** to those on the dock as the cruise ship began its voyage.

Write two sentences. Use **waive** in one and **wave** in the other.

167

© 2003 J. Weston Walch, Publisher

waive, wave

Wave can be a noun as well as a verb.

wave (n)—a disturbance on the surface of a liquid body in the form of a moving ridge; any surging moment resembling a wave, as of a feeling, an opinion, or a tendency

Example: Dylan, a professional surfer, rode the high **waves** at Hawaii's most popular beach.

Circle the proper word to make the sentence correct.

1. A (waive, wave) of concern came over the crowd as the team trailed in the last inning.

2. Students (waive, wave) their civil rights upon entering a school building.

3. The typhoon created such huge (waives, waves) that people near the coast were evacuated.

4. Trevor suffered a (waive, wave) of nausea when he had to dissect a frog in biology class.

5. The crowd (waived, waved) to Britney as she left the concert stage.

6. I will not (waive, wave) my right to a trial by a jury of my peers.

168

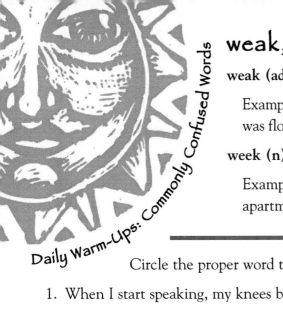

weak, week

weak (adj)—not strong; frail; lacking vigor; delicate

Example: The **weak** connection eventually broke, and the basement was flooded.

week (n)—a period of seven successive days

Example: Helen paid $200 a **week** to rent her one-bedroom apartment.

Circle the proper word to make the sentence correct.

1. When I start speaking, my knees become (weak, week) and begin to buckle.

2. All right, so you caught me at a (weak, week) moment, and I lent you the money.

3. Jan had been notified every day for a (weak, week) that her mortgage was past due.

4. I expect to hear about my college acceptance a (weak, week) from today.

169

weather, whether

weather (n, adj)—the state of the atmosphere with respect to wind, temperature, clouding, moisture, pressure, and so forth; a weathercast

> Example: Darren listened to the **weather** forecast before he decided to fly home.

> Example: The **weather** was bright and clear as the hikers continued their journey.

weather (v)—to expose to the weather; to age or discolor by the weather; to bear up against and come safely through a storm or trouble

> Example: The wind and rain **weathered** the natural wood of the cabin.

> **whether (conj)**—used to introduce the first of two alternatives, and sometimes repeated before the second alternative, usually with *or*; used to introduce a single alternative, the other being implied or understood

> > Example: **Whether** or not we have finished the project is still undecided.

170

Write one sentence using all four words above. You will have to be creative, and your sentence may have to be quite long.

weather, whether

When talking about the **weather,** the following trick may be helpful:

The w<u>ea</u>ther was cl<u>ea</u>r.

Circle the correct words in the following paragraph.

It really mattered (weather, whether) or not the (weather, whether) would break so the golf tournament could continue. The final decision would be based on (weather, whether) the lightning stopped. The (weather, whether) for the entire four-day tournament had been bad, and there had been some doubt as to (weather, whether) play could even begin. However, by noon, the (weather, whether) had begun to clear, and all rain had stopped. (Weather, Whether) the soft fairways and soggy greens would affect play was the question. In any case, the golfers (weathered, whethered) the storm and continued to play with better (weather, whether) promised for the rest of the day. The only remaining question was (weather, whether) Tiger Woods could defend his title as Masters champion.

171

which, witch

which (adj, pronoun)—the particular one or ones

Example: Brian had difficulty deciding **which** fishing rod to buy. (adj)

Example: His decision was based upon **which** of the rods came with a reel. (pronoun)

witch (n)—a woman who practices sorcery; an ugly, old, vicious woman

Example: In Salem, Massachusetts, there is an active coven of **witches.**

Write two sentences. Use *which* in one and *witch* in the other. Exchange your sentences with a classmate. Decide which form of **which,** adjective or pronoun, he or she used. Then write your own sentence using the form of **which** that your classmate did not use. Return sentences, and read your classmate's sentence, making sure he or she used the correct form.

172

which, witch

People often confuse these two words, especially if they are hurrying. Think of a trick to help you remember how to use each word. Share your ideas with classmates.

Circle the proper word to make the sentence correct. Then, at the end of each sentence, write the part of speech of the word you circled.

1. I always had difficulty deciding (which, witch) dessert I liked best.
   _____

2. You have given me several reasons, none of (which, witch) is acceptable.
   _____

3. The children were afraid of the old woman because they thought she was a (which, witch). _____

4. (Which, Witch) of these suits do you like better, the brown or the blue?
   _____

5. In Shakespeare's *Macbeth*, the (whiches, witches) tell Macbeth several prophecies. _____

173

whose, who's

whose (adj, pronoun)—the possessive form of *who* that indicates ownership

> Example: I don't care **whose** book this is; it needs to be covered. (adj)

> Example: Mary, **whose** raincoat was missing, got soaked on the first day of school. (pronoun)

who's—contraction of *who is*

> Example: **Who's** the winner of the raffle?

Circle the proper word to make the sentence correct.

1. Janice is the sophomore (whose, who's) representing the class at the board meeting.

2. Noah is the soccer player (whose, who's) jersey number is 62.

3. We need to know (whose, who's) fault the accident was so we can initiate legal action.

4. Tell me, (whose, who's) the one who put that graffiti on the back wall of the school?

5. We don't know (whose, who's) going to be the center on the basketball team.

174

whose, who's

People often confuse these two words. The easiest way to remember which term to use is to make sure that **whose** shows ownership. If you are using **who's,** replace it with *who is* or *who has* and see if your sentence still makes sense.

Write a paragraph using **whose** and **who's** at least five times each.

175

woman, women

woman (n)—an adult female human

Example: Madeleine Albright was the first **woman** to serve as United States Secretary of State.

women (n)—the plural form of *woman*

Example: Two of the **women** in the band played guitar.

Circle the proper word to make the sentence correct.

1. Gwyneth Paltrow is one of the (woman, women) in show business who has succeeded both on stage and in movies.

2. Four (woman, women) in the United States Senate are from California and Maine.

3. (Woman, Women) have fought for years to receive equal pay for equal work.

4. Eleanor Roosevelt was one (woman, women) highly admired by the American public.

Write two sentences of your own. Use **woman** in one and **women** in the other.

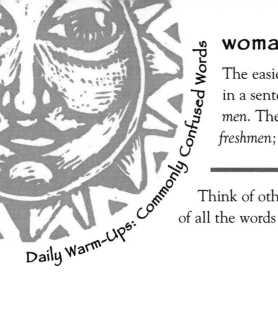

woman, women

The easiest way to decide whether you should use **woman** or **women** in a sentence is to remember that the rule is the same for *man* and *men*. The rule applies to other words ending in *man* and *men*: *freshman, freshmen; gentleman, gentlemen; fireman, firemen*.

Think of other words for which the *man/men* rule applies. Generate a list of all the words you can think of and share your list with classmates.

177

your, you're

your (adj)—the possessive form of *you* that indicates ownership

Example: Please place all of **your** books on the floor before we begin the test.

you're—contraction of *you are*

Example: There is no question that **you're** going to do well in the debate.

Circle the correct words in the following paragraph.

(Your, You're) not always sure of (your, you're) own abilities, especially when every time you do something using (your, you're) own talent, (your, you're) immediately criticized for using (your, you're) creativity. As you get older and more experienced, however, (your, you're) confidence will be renewed, and (your, you're) going to believe in (your, you're) approach to (your, you're) own original artwork. Trust me, (your, you're) going to be a very successful artist in whatever medium you choose.

your, you're

People often mistake these two words. A good way to decide which term is correct to use is to replace the word with *you are*. If *you are* makes sense in your sentence, you should use *you're*. If it does not make sense, you should use *your*, which shows ownership.

Look through any documents that you have available—old homework papers, old tests, essays, and so forth. The documents can also be pieces that you haven't written. For example, you may have a letter from your principal or a teacher. Peruse these documents for any uses of **your** and **you're.** Check to see if they are used correctly. If not, use a pencil to write in the correct word.

179

Review

Circle the proper term to make the sentence correct.

1. Telephone poles are (stationary, stationery) and are placed along the sides of the street.

2. Can you tell me (whose, who's) going to the carnival during the Fourth of July weekend?

3. They packed the car with all of (their, there, they're) gear for mountain climbing.

4. The men sat on one side of the hall and the (woman, women) on the other.

5. My headache is so severe that I feel as though my head is in a (vice, vise).

6. Tell me what (your, you're) going to be doing this weekend.

7. (Which, Witch) one of you is riding with me?

8. I can't decide (weather, whether) I should go to the dance or to the movies.

180

1. 1. accepted 2. accept 3. except 4. accept
    5. except
2. Sentences will vary.
3. 1. advice 2. advice 3. advice 4. advise
4. 1. advised 2. advice 3. advise 4. advice
    Sentences will vary.
5. 1. affect 2. effects 3. effect
6. 1. effected 2. affect 3. affected
    Sentences will vary.
7. 1. I'll 2. I'll 3. aisle 4. I'll
8. 1. isle 2. aisle 3. Isle 4. aisle
9. 1. all ready 2. already 3. All ready 4. already
10. 1. all ready 2. All ready 3. already 4. already
11. 1. all together 2. altogether 3. all together
    4. altogether 5. altogether
12. Sentences will vary.
13. alluded; allude; eluding; allude; elude; alluded;
    eluding; eluded
14. 1. allusions 2. illusion 3. illusion 4. illusion
15. 1. allusions 2. Illusions 3. illusion
    4. allusions

16. 1. altar 2. altars 3. alter 4. alter
17. altar; altered; alter; alter; alter
18. 1. Among 2. between 3. between 4. among
19. 1. among 2. Among 3. between 4. Among
20. angry with; mad; mad; angry
21. mad; angry with; madness; mad; mad; mad
22. 1. Ante 2. anti 3. anti 4. Ante 5. anti
23. 1. apprised 2. appraised 3. appraising
    4. apprise 5. appraise
24. 1. as 2. as 3. like 4. As
25. 1. As 2. like 3. like 4. as
26. 1. essays 2. assayed 3. assayed 4. essays
27. 1. essays 2. essay 3. essayed; assaying
    4. Essay
28. 1. bad 2. bad 3. badly 4. bad
29. 1. bad 2. badly 3. badly 4. bad
30. 1. as 2. accepted; elude 3. I'll; all together
    4. illusion 5. affect 6. advise 7. bad; apprised
    8. assayed; essay
31. base; bass; bass; base
32. bass; base; bass; base; base

Daily Warm-Ups: Commonly Confused Words

33. 1. because 2. since 3. since 4. because
34. 1. since 2. because 3. Because 4. Since
35. Sentences will vary.
36. Sentences will vary.
37. 1. boor 2. boar 3. boor
38. 1. bore 2. bored 3. bore 4. bore
39. 1. Born 2. borne 3. born 4. borne
40. 1. brake 2. break 3. break 4. braked
41. 1. break 2. brakes 3. break 4. break
42. by; buy; by; by
43. by; bye; buy; by; by
44. 1. capital 2. capital 3. capitol
45. 1. capital 2. capitol 3. capital
46. cent; scent; scent
47. sent; sent; scent; cent
48. 1. choose 2. chose 3. chooses 4. choosing
     5. chose
49. Sentences will vary.
50. Sentences will vary.
51. sight; site; cited; sighted; site; sight; sighted;
     site

52. 1. cliques 2. clicks 3. Cliques 4. cliques
53. Sentences will vary.
54. Sentences will vary.
55. clos; clos; clos; cloz; clos; cloz
56. 1. cloths 2. clothes 3. cloths 4. clothes
57. 1. clothe 2. cloths 3. clothe 4. clothes
58. course; coarse; course; coarse; course; course
59. 1. course 2. course 3. course 4. course;
     course
60. 1. Since 2. based; bass 3. borne 4. brakes;
     bore 5. capital 6. sent; scent 7. choose; site
     8. clique; clothes
61. 1. compliment 2. complement 3. comple-
     ment 4. compliment 5. Complementary
62. 1. complemented 2. complimented
     3. complement
     Sentences will vary.
63. Tricks and paragraphs will vary.
64. 1. confident 2. confidant 3. confident
     4. confident

65. 1. conscious 2. conscience 3. conscience
    4. conscious 5. conscious
66. Sentences will vary.
67. council; counsel; consul; council; council;
    council; consul; counsel; council
68. Sentences will vary.
69. descent; decent; descent; dissent; decent;
    dissented; decent
70. Sentences will vary.
71. 1. deserted 2. deserts 3. dessert 4. deserted
    5. desert
72. 1. device 2. device 3. devise 4. devise
73. Paragraphs will vary.
74. 1. dew 2. due 3. do 4. due 5. Do
75. Sentences will vary.
76. Sentences will vary.
77. 1. doesn't 2. doesn't 3. doesn't 4. don't
    5. don't
78. Paragraphs will vary.
79. 1. duels 2. dueled 3. dual 4. duel 5. dual

80. 1. each other 2. one another 3. one another
    4. each other
81. Sentences will vary.
82. Sentences will vary.
83. 1. elicit 2. illicit 3. elicited 4. illicit
84. Sentences will vary.
85. eminent; imminent; eminent; imminent;
    eminent; eminent; eminent
86. 1. envelopes 2. envelops 3. envelop
    4. envelopes
87. Sentences will vary.
88. 1. evoked 2. evoked 3. evokes 4. invoked
    5. Invoking
89. Sentences will vary.
90. 1. compliment; dessert 2. conscience;
    conscious; illicit 3. confident; each other
    4. fare 5. doesn't; different from
    6. dissent; council 7. imminent 8. devise; due
91. Sentences will vary.

Daily Warm-Ups: Commonly Confused Words

92. 1. further 2. further 3. farther 4. farther
    5. further
93. Sentences will vary.
94. 1. fewer 2. less 3. fewer 4. Fewer 5. less
    6. fewer
95. 1. flair 2. flares 3. flare 4. flared
96. Tricks and paragraphs will vary.
97. 1. formerly 2. formally 3. formerly
    4. formally 5. Formerly
98. Paragraphs will vary.
99. 1. fourth 2. correct 3. forth 4. correct
    5. correct, forth
100. Paragraphs will vary.
101. 1. good 2. well 3. well 4. good 5. well
102. Sentences will vary.
103. 1. great 2. great 3. grating 4. grate 5. grated
104. Sentences will vary.
105. hanged; hanged; hung; hung; hung; hung;
     hanged
106. Sentences will vary.

107. 1. have 2. correct 3. have 4. have 5. correct
     6. have
108. Paragraphs will vary.
109. 1. hear 2. hear 3. here 4. Hear 5. here
     6. hear
110. Sentences will vary.
111. 1. horde 2. hoarded 3. correct 4. hoard
     5. correct
112. Sentences will vary.
113. 1. hole 2. hole 3. holes 4. whole 5. holes
     6. whole
114. Sentences will vary.
115. idylls; idols; idle; idyll; idle; idol; idyll; idled;
     idle
116. Tricks and paragraphs will vary.
117. 1. infer 2. implying 3. imply 4. inferred
     5. infer 6. infer
118. 1. its 2. It's 3. its 4. It's; its; its
119. 1. It's 2. its 3. its 4. its
     Paragraphs will vary.

120. 1. It's; here 2. imply; further 3. hung; hole
     4. fourth 5. hoard; fewer 6. idol; well
     7. have 8. great
121. 1. lay 2. lie 3. lie 4. laid
122. 1. lay 2. lay 3. lain 4. laid
     Sentences will vary.
123. 1. led 2. lead 3. led 4. led
     Sentences will vary.
124. 1. lead 2. lead 3. lead 4. lead
     Paragraphs will vary.
125. *Literally* should be changed to *figuratively* in
     every instance it is used in the paragraph.
126. Sentences will vary.
127. lose; loose; losing; loose; loose; lose; loose;
     losing; losing; losing
128. 1. loosely 2. losing 3. loose 4. correct
     5. loser 6. lose
     Sentences will vary.
129. 1. medal 2. meddle 3. medal
     Sentences will vary.

130. 1. medals 2. meddle 3. mettle 4. meddled
     5. mettle
131. 1. past 2. passed 3. passed 4. past
132. 1. past (adj) 2. past (noun) 3. passed (verb)
     4. past (adj)
133. 1. personnel 2. personal 3. personal
     4. personnel
134. Definitions will vary.
     1. personnel 2. personal 3. personnel
     4. personal
135. Sentences will vary.
136. principal; principles; principles; principles;
     principal; principal; principal
137. 1. quiet (adj) 2. quite (adv) 3. quiet (noun)
     4. quite (adv); quite (adv)
138. 1. quieted 2. quieted 3. quite 4. Quiet
     Sentences will vary.
139. Sentences will vary.
140. 1. rise 2. raise 3. raising 4. rise 5. raised
     6. rise Tricks will vary.

141. Sentences will vary.
142. Tricks will vary.
     1. recently 2. resents; recent 3. recent
     4. correct 5. correct
143. Paragraphs will vary.
144. right; writes; right; writes; rite; rite; right
145. Sentences will vary.
146. 1. scene 2. Seen 3. seen 4. scene 5. scene
     6. seen
147. 1. set 2. sat 3. sit 4. Set 5. set 6. sits
148. Paragraphs will vary.
149. Sentences will vary.
150. 1. lose 2. lain 3. sit 4. principal 5. passed
     6. right 7. quite; scene 8. led
151. Paragraphs will vary.
152. 1. stairs 2. stares 3. stared 4. stairs 5. stares
     Sentences will vary.
153. 1. stationary 2. stationary 3. stationery
     4. stationery 5. stationery 6. stationary
154. Tricks will vary.

155. Sentences will vary.
156. 1. steel 2. steal 3. steal 4. steal 5. steel;
     stealing 6. steel
157. 1. than 2. then 3. than 4. than 5. then
158. Paragraphs will vary.
159. Sentences will vary.
160. their; they're; there; their; their; there; their;
     they're; they're
161. Documents will vary.
162. too; to; two; Too; too; two; too; two; to; two; to
163. 1. vice 2. vice 3. vise 4. vices 5. vice
     Sentences will vary.
164. Tricks and examples of vices will vary.
165. Paragraphs will vary.
166. 1. wasted (verb) 2. waste (noun) 3. waist
     (noun) 4. Waste (adj) 5. waste (noun)
167. Sentences will vary.
168. 1. wave 2. waive 3. waves 4. wave 5. waved
     6. waive
169. 1. weak 2. weak 3. week 4. week

Daily Warm-Ups: Commonly Confused Words

170. Sentences will vary.
171. whether; weather; whether; weather; whether;
     weather; Whether; weathered; weather;
     whether
172. Sentences will vary.
173. Tricks will vary.
     1. which (adj) 2. which (pronoun)
     3. witch (noun) 4. Which (pronoun)
     5. witches (noun)
174. 1. who's 2. whose 3. whose 4. who's 5. who's
175. Paragraphs will vary.
176. 1. women 2. women 3. Women 4. woman
     Sentences will vary.
177. Lists of words will vary.
178. You're; your; your; you're; your; your; you're;
     your; your; you're
179. Documents will vary.
180. 1. stationary 2. who's 3. their 4. women
     5. vise 6. you're 7. Which 8. whether

Turn downtime into learning time!

Other books in the

Daily Warm-Ups series:

- Algebra
- Analogies
- Biology
- Critical Thinking
- Earth Science
- Geography
- Geometry
- Journal Writing
- Mythology

- Poetry
- Pre-Algebra
- Shakespeare
- Spelling & Grammar
- Test-Prep Words
- U.S. History
- Vocabulary
- World History
- Writing